Susan in the City

The *Cambridge News* Years

Susan Grossey

ISBN: 1544182619
ISBN-13: 978-1544182612

Susan's website:
www.susangrossey.wordpress.com

Susan's writing blog:
www.susangrossey.wordpress.com/current-project-blog

Susan's other books:

📖 "Fatal Forgery"
📖 "The Man in the Canary Waistcoat"
📖 "Worm in the Blossom"
📖 "Portraits of Pretence"
📖 plus a shelf-load of books on anti-money laundering
(Susan's day job)

DEDICATION

To all the lovely readers of "Susan in the City"
who loyally put up with my ramblings
every Monday for a decade

CONTENTS

Introduction   i

Health   1

Food and shopping   21

Transport   43

Human behaviour   75

Home life   103

Cambridge   137

INTRODUCTION

Back in the summer of 2006, I went out to lunch with a friend. He was moaning about his job and I asked him what, if he had the pick of anything in the world, he would like to do to make his living. "I'd like a weekly column in a newspaper," he said, "where I could hold forth on whatever I like." We threw the idea around a bit, and I suggested that expecting take-up by a national broadsheet right off the bat was probably a bit optimistic but that he should approach our local paper and see if they were interested. He was of the view that you can't just call up an editor and offer to write for him, so we made a bet: I would contact the *Cambridge Evening News* (as it was then) and try to persuade them to give me a weekly column, and if I succeeded, he would pay me a tenner.

I'm still waiting for the tenner, but the journalistic planets must have been in alignment that day because the editor said I could have a six-month trial. And after six months, we just carried on – for ten years. This book is a selection of eighty of those columns (I wrote five hundred and ten in total), representing what I think is the best of the decade.

1 HEALTH

This was the very first column published under the "Susan in the City" byline, on Wednesday 9 August 2006. After a few weeks I was moved to my permanent home in the Monday edition.

Boswelox babes

9 August 2006

This year I celebrated one of those birthdays ending in 0 – and not one of the good ones, either. Several cards were received suggesting life begins at this point, which gave me ample opportunity to test my new shredder.

My attitude to my age ricochets wildly between a rather feisty "take me as I am – older women are more interesting anyway" and a more whiny "what have I done with my life – by my age, Marilyn Monroe had made thirty movies of varying quality, married three men of even more varying quality and died in a gorgeously naked manner". I am now officially too old to die young, and am definitely in Miss Jean Brodie territory – in my prime, I mean, not in Edinburgh.

In my darker moments (usually when I've filled in one of those forms where you have to indicate your age and the last option is "40 or over") I find myself drawn to those ridiculous displays of "age-defying" products that cram the aspirational shelves of Boots. Daughter of a mathematician and married to an engineer, I should know enough basic science to dismiss the very idea of skin-based time-travel, but wishful thinking can be more compelling than logic.

Foolishly I bought one of those powerful magnifying mirrors, which turns my skin into parched, dried-out acres gouged by wrinkles you could lose a camel train in. When I peer really closely, I can almost see the dreaded free radicals cavorting and multiplying in delight – they sound like the good guys, awash with right-on sixties terminology, but don't be fooled.

In real life I am an averagely decisive person, but in potion-world I turn into an Olympic standard ditherer. Should I be trying to maintain, enhance, rejuvenate or age-defy? Milk, lotion, gel, cream or masque? Day, night or both? It's just as well I don't wear make-up too, or I'd have to give up work, abandon my husband and set up camp under the No 7 counter in Boots just to have time for all the choices.

I would ask for advice from those scarily superior ladies in bright white coats, but I'm frightened they would turn me into a clone of themselves and then convince me that Boswelox really works – and I'm only forty, not demented.

Fogging up the gardens

2 July 2006

A recent report put out by the Department of Health (which seems to spend all its time generating statistics rather than cures) tells us that a quarter of adults in Cambridge are smokers. And I thought this was an intelligent town. However, the day of the non-smoker is finally upon us – together we have risen up and banned you puffers from our restaurants and our pubs and our offices.

Smoking is a total mystery to me. Young women spend a fortune on shampoo, body wash and perfume to make themselves smell like roses or tangerines or Victoria Beckham (who actually looks like a tangerine rather than smelling like one, and a petulant tangerine at that), and then overlay it all with a mobile cloud of fag smoke. When I was a teenager all the lads smoked – which was great, as it meant they each had one less hand to wheedle its way up your skirt or down your jumper. I imagine they thought the casual fag made them look like Clint Eastwood in the no name movies, but for most of them, Dot Cotton was nearer the mark. Some of them even kept a cigarette pack tucked in the sleeve of their t-shirts, aping Marlon Brando, and then wondered how their mums knew they'd been smoking – apparently t-shirts hold the shape of what has last been in them, which is how my husband can tell from the lumpy bits on the front that I've been wearing his white t-shirts as vests.

SUSAN IN THE CITY

So as of yesterday we are now Smoke Free Britain. Hah. I've seen this in action already in Ireland and the Channel Islands, and all that happens is that the smokers move a nanometre outside the premises, and you have to fight your way through a fug tunnel to get in. They also colonise all the best seats outside, so you get a smoke-free atmosphere indoors while sitting in the pub garden is like sucking on the exhaust pipe of a bus. And does it mean that waiters and barmen will now be joining the legions of British workers who already use up 65% of their working day getting from their desks to the outside, having a fag break and then making their way back indoors? In some tall buildings and inaccessible government offices, that can be an epic journey requiring crampons and (oh the irony) oxygen tanks.

As a result of this column I was invited onto the Jeremy Vine show on Radio 2. My on-air combatant was "Sunday Times journalist and prominent smoker" Rod Liddle, whose first comment to me was "What a silly woman you are!". I rallied in my best Joyce Grenfell tones, and even extracted what I am told is a very rare apology from Mr Liddle. But before I get too puffed up with my own national media persona, I should confess that the show's researcher told me that she had great difficulty tracking me down: "I called the Cambridge Evening News and the lady on the front desk said she'd never heard of you because she only reads the important bits of the paper."

Counting calories

21 April 2008

Listening to the radio this morning I had to check my calendar to make sure it wasn't April Fools' Day, for apparently there are moves a-foot in America to force restaurateurs to indicate on their menus the calorific content of each dish. Quite apart from the fact that mathematicians have yet to discover numbers large enough for some American meals (any culture that can sustain a whole chain of scofferies called The Cheesecake Factory is obviously at ease with piggery), can you imagine anything worse? I once had a female colleague who kept a "calorie diary" in which she noted everything she ate, which wasn't much. We eventually shut her in a filing cabinet (under I for Irritating) and she didn't have the strength to push open the drawer.

I should confess from the outset that I am among the 0.038% of British women who are not currently on a diet, and the 0.0000056% who have never been on one. (*Made-up statistics, 2008*) Personally, I have always found that as soon as I deny myself any foodstuff, I can hardly breathe, sleep or function for thinking about and craving that item. No crisps until Friday, I declare on Monday morning. By Tuesday evening I am having indecent fantasies about Mr Pringle and his natty bow-tie. By Thursday morning, I would turn down a date with Jeremy Paxman if the alternative was a large bowl of smoky bacon crisps, and by Thursday evening even Sean Connery would be getting the flick (unless he came equipped with some cheesy Wotsits, which I suspect he does).

And as I have the moral fibre of a "team player" on "The Apprentice", I have learnt that diets involving abstinence are not for me. Instead, I opt for plea bargaining. If I have two chocolate biscuits at elevenses, I won't have any in the afternoon. Unfortunately, low sugar levels after lunch often adversely affect my biscuit-related memory. If anyone's keeping count at that great Weight Watchers' meeting in the sky, I won't be able to eat at all in 2009 in order to make good on all my deals.

So rather than dieting and calorie-counting, I use more practical indicators of my chubbiness. If my jeans won't do up on the first wear after washing, I blame it on shrinkage. If they won't do up after that, even when I lie on the floor and heave at the zip with a coat-hanger, I put them back in the wardrobe and wear a skirt instead. Problem solved. Pass the biscuits.

It was about this time that my editor told me that he had entered me for an award for Columnist of the Year in the Press Gazette Regional Newspaper Awards. Reader, I did not even make the shortlist of seven. The award was won by Colin Drury, then of the "Halifax Evening Courier". He now freelances for publications such as the "Guardian" and the "Independent", who doubtless poached him because of his CotY award, but I'm not bitter at all. Not at all.

Flu-san in the City

23 November 2009

Not since I slipped on a pair of synthetic leg-warmers and knotted my long t-shirt at the side in about 1980 have I been a dedicated follower of fashion. But this week I am bang on trend: I have flu. And before you ask, no, I do not know whether it is porcine or ordinary. I did the rather scary online questionnaire provided by NHS Direct – is the name ironic, given that the website is liberally scattered with warnings not to get in direct contact with anyone, in particular your doctor or pharmacist, but to hole up at home, paint a red cross on the door and get used to the poisonous company of Jeremy Kyle and Judge Judy. The questionnaire confirmed that I do not have meningitis or heart failure and that I am not pregnant, and concluded that it is possible that I have swine flu. The miracle of modern technology: my cat could have told me that.

My next recommended step was to find a "flu friend". Puh-lease. I looked so bad when I opened the door to the postman that he leapt to the other side of the street and frisbeed my letters to me, so quite who is going to volunteer to be my friend I do not know. This elusive friend can then go to the pharmacy and collect my Tamiflu. The website explains, with touching candour, that Tamiflu does not cure flu: it reduces its duration by about a day, and may bring on some colourful side effects such as "violent vomiting". I'm not a decisive person at the best of times, and my flu-addled brain was so incapable of weighing up the options that eventually it was all too late, as Tamiflu has to be taken at the first signs of flu – not when your husband is renegotiating the "how long I have to stay in mourning" bit of the marriage contract. (Forever. Yes, really.)

Poor old chap – I am not an easy patient. No stoic, I think I am dying at least three times a day. I conceive desperate cravings for unsuitable foods (violet crème chocolates – perhaps this is an ancient folk remedy) and insist on watching "comforting" programmes (I made my way through the whole of "The Forsyte Saga", although it did worry me a bit when young Jolyon succumbed to typhoid...). Quick: what does NHS Direct say about typhoid?

Handy tips for milking a manicure

6 September 2010

As the title of this column suggests that I should keep up with developments in our fair city, I decided – purely selflessly, you understand – to try out the new Sanctuary Spa on the top floor of the Grand Arcade. I know: it's a filthy job, etc. Like its big sister in London, the SS – ah, no, let's not use that – the SSpa is only for ladies. (A phrase ruined forever for me by the boys from "Little Britain", but in this case, it's true.) I'm not generally in favour of gender segregation, but there is something to be said for a single-sex spa environment. At home I have to put up with regular comments about my "array of unguents" and my "pots of gloop", so it's nice to dither over the relative merits of a lactogel peel and a pro-lift firming facial without the raised eyebrows (that's another treatment entirely).

In the end, I opted for a youth boosting manicure, which you don't want to be ordering after a few Martinis. I won't go into the digital details, but it was jolly nice, with plinky-plonk music in the background, a light scent of lavender in the air, and my gnarled claws toasting gently inside warming mitts. Fancying myself very swish, I even insisted on paying beforehand, as I once read in a magazine that if you pay afterwards you ruin the polish by delving into your purse – darlings, stick with me and you'll learn all the tricks of elegant living. Sadly, the magazine did not explain how to tackle a bike lock after a manicure, so I had to waylay a nice chap in the underground bike park and ask for his help.

And this – it turns out – is the real benefit of getting a manicure. OK, so your skin feels bit softer and you can sport nails of an unnatural colour, but the best thing of all is the sheer helplessness it visits upon you. For days afterwards I was able to walk around waving my hands pathetically like a baby bird with a broken wing, saying, "Please can someone empty the dishwasher [insert dreaded task of choice] – I don't want to ruin my nails". I may get one every week – or at least every time I think we need to change the duvet cover. And imagine if I were to get a pedicure too… Tell me, can you still order sedan chairs?

Galvanised by my own vitamins

21 February 2011

Everyone I meet at the moment seems to be clutching tissues and nasal sprays, or coughing like a miner with a 60-a-day habit. As I make my living by talking I am particularly keen to steer clear of sore throats, and so I try to defend myself with a battery of vitamins.

When I was little, vitamins were just coming into vogue, and my mum daringly started giving me Haliborange. As I didn't have unlimited access to sweeties in those days (I got 40p pocket money per week, and always spent it on *The Beano*, a packet of WigWams, and a Walnut Whip for my mum), I grew to love these shockingly bright orange tablets, which supposedly contained as much vitamin C as half of Florida. And as I frequently pinched them from the cupboard, I was a stranger to scurvy. But in truth, 1976 was probably the last time I really understood the vitamin concept. Since then, things have moved way beyond me.

If you go into Boots now, there are at least three aisles dedicated to all sorts of supplements – pills, tablets, gelatine-free capsules and, for all I know, tipped darts for the reluctant convert. It's a bit like reading the family medical dictionary: you start to imagine that you've got it all. Maybe I do need stronger teeth and glossier hair – oh, hold on, I think I've strayed into the pet section by mistake. What is Omega 3 – and what happened to Omegas 1 and 2? Do I really want to take something fizzy to dance in the streets and be me but better? What about swallowing one giant tablet with everything I need in it – or is that basically an apple? And now that I'm 45, should I be looking at those boxes with the ethereal smiling lady on them – to judge by the offering, menopause will be a mixture of walking through wildflower meadows and dashing desperately to the nearest loo.

For three weeks, I have been pestering everyone about a lingering metallic taste in my mouth. I've read dozens of online articles, suggesting that the culprit could be a deteriorating filling, or pine nuts (I kid you not), or that it's all in my head (which is where I keep my mouth, oddly enough). But I've solved the mystery myself: it's my snuffle-busting zinc tablets, which I take religiously all winter. It seems that I have galvanised myself.

Hip, hip hooray for hospital

14 March 2011

My husband recently had an operation. (I wasn't going to specify but he says you'll all be assuming that I've had him done, so I'd better clarify that it was something to do with his hip, which he wore out by playing too much sport and generally being Extremely Manly and Devilishly Virile.) Anyway, it gave us an opportunity to sample the inpatient facilities at a large local hospital (first letter A, last letter S). And despite all the wailing media reports about the NHS going to hell in an MRSA-infected handcart, we found it jolly nice: friendly staff, decent food, sparkly new hip. But as someone who is thankfully unfamiliar with hospitals, a few things struck me.

First of all, the whole site (every building, every floor) is stuffed with vending machines selling the usual selection of sugary drinks and fattening snacks. Now, I realise that the NHS needs to make money where it can, and I share the philosophy of a friend of mine who is an oncologist: it's bad enough being ill without having to survive on nettle soup and knitted wholemeal yoghurt, so eat whatever you fancy. But surely it is sending out mixed messages for a hospital to offer such abundant calorific naughtiness – including a full-service burger bar in the food court.

Secondly, rather like airports it seems that hospitals are self-sufficient communities. This one has a bank, a travel agency, a dry cleaner's and a solicitor's office (expert in wills and malpractice suits, I assume) as well as a hairdresser and numerous shops. With the thousands of staff, plentiful beds and the neighbouring maternity facilities, you could probably hunker down here during a nuclear winter and set about repopulating the world (or at least East Anglia).

Thirdly, the hospital site is possibly the ugliest place I have visited for quite some time. I know it's winter and I know it's a functional environment, but would a few flowering shrubs or walls in a colour other than prison grey go amiss? (Actually, I've visited a prison and their walls were mauve – apparently it calms the more fractious inmates. Apparently.)

And lastly, why are the gowns (which is, frankly, a misleadingly elegant term for a large hankie with tie-cords) all printed liberally with "For hospital use only"? Do people really become so addicted to parading around bare-bottomed that they pinch them (the gowns, not the bottoms)?

A good walk walked

20 May 2013

It's that time of year again, as the drakes chase the ducks along the river and the trees burst forth into bud, for my husband to dig out his golf clubs from the furthest recesses of the garage and declare, "I fancy a quick nine holes!" Growing up in Singapore when there were no public golf courses (land area 274 square miles + population 5.3 million = real estate prices astronomical), I never learned how to play. Husband, on the other hand, earned teenage pocket money working as a caddy for rich people in golf-laden Surrey. Moreover, he is genetically wired to want to try every sport, while my genetic tug is to sofas and chocolate.

I don't want you to think that I haven't been on a golf course, for I have – many times. I disagree completely with Mark Twain's claim that golf is a good walk spoilt, as some of my finest walks have been on golf courses. They generally have good views and nice trees, and being essentially an urban creature I like to find that someone has mown the countryside for me. And golf courses can hold surprises. On one particularly posh one I was wandering around looking for lost balls in the rough when a man motored up to me in a golf cart and asked if I wanted an ice-cream. I should say so! Not nearly enough sports come with mid-event Cornettos. But my best ever course was a small seaside one (a links, I am told) in Portugal. It had a sort of ladder on wheels, rather like a set of aircraft steps, that you could position and then mount to get a clear view down an undulating fairway. Great fun was had by all, except the players following me. And in the clubhouse was a tubby Labrador who, for the promise of a share in a sandwich, would walk around the course with you. She and I had a good old natter and munch while he played.

Am I ever tempted to take a swing myself, you ask? Well, I shouldn't, of course, as I haven't paid to play – and that is the reason that I give to my husband whenever he offers a club. But the real reason, between you and me, is that I suspect that I would be really rather good at golf – outstanding, even – and that would play havoc with marital harmony.

Doctor not in the house

24 February 2014

Many years ago, when I was a callow young woman and entirely unsympathetic, I telephoned my mother-in-law and found her in tears. "It's Doctor Gooding," she sobbed. The family GP. Fully booked? Dead? Struck off? "No – he's retired!" Back then, I couldn't see the problem: all doctors go through the same training, they all know what the thigh bone connects to, so just sign up with his replacement and carry on. Dear MIL, please accept a long overdue apology for my lack of compassion, for the same calamity has just befallen me.

When I started at university in Cambridge, I toddled off to my college's recommended doctors' practice and was allocated "our newest GP – she's good with young women". And so she was: she was about a week older than me and had been qualified for twenty minutes, and as long as she pretended to be confident in what she was saying, I pretended to believe her. She got used to my imprecise symptoms – "I just feel a bit, you know, not right" – and I learnt not to save up all of my concerns for one visit, armed with a list as long as, well, my arm. And we matured together.

She no longer had to pretend to be confident as she turned into a fantastic GP. When I needed some gynaecological attention and went to a specialist clinic, I almost cried with relief when they said that I really should see the local expert in the matter, and then named my very own doctor. And when I moved to London for three years (forgive me – 'twas the madness of youth) I refused to register with a local practice and instead brought all of my sickness by train to the door of my beloved Cambridge GP.

I should have guessed, I suppose. The children in the photos on her windowsill kept growing, and then she talked about them leaving home. But it was the most ghastly shock to find, when I tried to book an appointment last week, that she has retired. It's a bit like contemplating a second marriage: can I really face going through all of my history again, and hoping that the new person is not too revolted? But I have no choice, and so I have signed up with her successor. At our first meeting, we eyed each other across the desk and, now wiser to the ways of the world, I asked that vital question: "Are you about to retire?"

Birthday rambles and brambles

11 August 2014

As regular readers will know, my husband turned fifty recently, and on his actual birthday he got to choose what we did. I offered a smorgasbord of options, from a boat trip on the Thames to a day in Southwold – and he elected to walk to Ely. So we took the bus to Swaffham Prior, clambered up onto Devil's Dyke, and set off. We attracted a few glances in Reach, as I own neither shorts nor trousers – nor indeed those peculiar halfway jobs – and so was walking in a pair of stout shoes, ankle socks, and a flowery dress.

Now, I like a nice walk – and even more so when there is a complete lack of mountains in the way. But what I had failed to factor in was the effect of the recent sunshine and showers on the path we used. The grass on it had grown like topsy, and it was like walking through sand – the luxuriant fronds grabbed at our feet with each step – and although I started out lifting my legs high like a dressage pony (actually, my legs are very like those of a dressage pony – sturdy is the word) that soon became too tiring. I then resorted to my tried and tested technique of foot-dragging and whining, which earned me a short sit-down in the shade of a weeping willow, and a muesli bar. Yes, dear reader: it was a warm day and so I had – for probably the first time ever – embarked on a journey of more than an hour without emergency chocolate.

SUSAN IN THE CITY

On we pressed towards Ely, the cathedral taunting us against the skyline – see how close I appear, and yet the signposts still say seven miles to go! We clambered over stiles into fields with big signs saying "Beware of the bull" and discovered that, city kids that we both are, we weren't entirely sure which was the bull and which his entirely blameless harem. We stared in astonishment as horseflies tore chunks out of our calves – apparently the name comes from their size, not their favoured target animal. And we waved cheerily as barges puttered past, their captains standing proudly at the stern, peaked caps at a jaunty angle and beer bellies baking in the sun.

After five hours we stumbled into Ely and fell face down into a cream tea at Peacock's – apologies to all other customers for the ripe country smells and loud snores emanating from our table.

Soon after this, I received the first of several very welcome and pleasant emails from my namesake (and age-sake) reader Sue Taylor. Over the next two years she supplied plenty of fodder for this column, and also revealed that although she uses the "Cambridge News" to line her rabbits' litter trays, "when I change the newspaper I always make sure that if I see your photo on the page, you are turned face down". Much appreciated.

2 FOOD AND SHOPPING

Horrorscopes

11 June 2007

One of the downsides of being literate is that I am drawn magnetically to glossy magazines. No matter that I tell myself that they have only five stock stories that they recycle endlessly. 1. How to get the man you want. 2. How to get rid of the man you didn't want after all. 3. How to be more assertive and get what you want. 4. How to be content with what you've got (be that a large rump, a boorish man or last season's curtains). And 5. How to look fabulous whatever your age, size, shape and personal style – fabulous, that is, according to the frankly bizarre standards of magazine fashion editors. Apparently white shifts over white leggings are in for the summer, which is bad news for those of us with a messy chocolate habit and the cellulite to prove it.

And it gets worse. Once I have such a magazine in my sweaty grasp, I cannot stop myself turning to the horoscope page. I am an educated woman. I have Biology O level, you know – albeit passed in 1982 when they taught us about reproduction by showing us flickery Super 8 films of rabbits in action, which has given me unrealistic expectations ever since. I live in a city boasting the world's most distinguished history of scientific discovery. And yet still I am willing, nay eager, to read the random ramblings of some fey fool called Marina von Marvell or Philippe Planete, dividing all six billion of us into twelve neat categories.

The key to a successful horoscope seems to be to write comments so bland that they could indeed apply to five hundred million people at once. "This month you will be irritated by someone close to you, but be patient and you'll reap the rewards." You're all nodding – ooh yes, that's me. (Unless you're Lady Sugar, of course: you can be as patient as a box of saints, my love, and Alan will never be anything less than monumentally irritating.) What I want is real, detailed guidance, along the lines of "On Tuesday 6th you will be invited to a party in Ipswich. Don't go, because the traffic on the A14 will be a nightmare, and that chap from Bournemouth will be there with his holiday snaps from Majorca and a desire to show everyone his unusual tan lines." After all, we Aquarians love to plan ahead.

Voucher vulture

17 November 2008

Shopping used to be so simple. You chose what you wanted, and paid the price on the sticky label. You didn't have to work out whether it was cheaper to buy three and get one free, or get interest-free credit and pay next October. And you didn't have to rootle through your collection of thirty-eight vouchers to see which would give you money off or extra points or chocolate sprinkles on top. In the past week, I have been sent "exciting offers" because I am a "valued customer" of a credit card, three chain stores, an airline and (mystifyingly, unless my cat has been surfing the Internet in my absence and pressed the wrong option) a dog-food company.

The problem is then where to keep this paper-based excitement. I used to stuff them into my purse, but unless I remembered to clear them out regularly, I had Tony Robinson and the Time Team lot on the doorstep looking for evidence of an ancient culture based on barter and bogof.

But the sad truth is that I am a sucker for these offers. I try to remind myself that it's only a bargain if you wanted it in the first place, but it's no good. So when Boots kindly gave me a voucher for £5 off anything from the Olay range, designed to fight the seven signs of aging, there I was, scouring the shelves. And not a moment too soon, it turns out, as I was exhibiting all seven signs. It took me a moment to remember why I had gone into the shop in the first place (sign 1), and then on being confronted with the serried ranks of lotions and potions I tutted and muttered, "Why are there so many? Too much choice these days…" (2). I bent down to look at one particular item and made the "oop aahh" noise on the way back up (3), holding the bottle at arm's-length so that I could read the ingredients (4). "Why did they have to rename it Olay? What was wrong with Ulay? It was good enough for my grandma," I wondered (5). Then I saw the price and gasped – £15.99 for a bit of gloopy face cream? (6) And finally I went to pay for it and realised that I had left my purse at home (7). Sadly, I think Olay's claims to address all of these may be over-ambitious.

Buy none, get two free

23 February 2009

I've talked before about how you need a calculator to go shopping these days, with all the BOGOFs and "threefers" making it tricky to work out how much it's all costing. And now the contagion has spread from the pre-scoff stage (i.e. supermarket decisions) to the post-cook stage (i.e. restaurants). What with *Explorer* magazine vouchers, offers on the Local Secrets website, tokens printed in this very publication, and flyers pushed through the door, I'm sure that it's only matter of time before I figure out a combination that will allow me to go out for a slap-up dinner, collect payment from the waiter, and get the maitre d' to give me a lift home on the back of his moped.

I think Pizza Express started it all. It was quite mild to begin with: buy four pizzas and get a garlic bread to share. Then the post-Christmas, pre-Valentine's lull kicked in. Restaurant managers throughout the town gazed round at deserted tables, and upped the ante. Buy a pizza, get a small glass of wine. Buy two main courses, get the cheaper one free. And now: buy two main courses, get the more expensive one free. My moment has come. Despite my many pretension to grandeur I'm a simple soul, and a plain margarita pizza is my very favourite – in essence, it's a bit of bread with tomato and cheese on it, and costs about five quid. My husband, on the other hand, has a more demanding palate: he likes the special pizza dough inflated with fairy breath then smeared with a rare cheese hand-churned by gentlewomen from a minor European royal dynasty and overlaid with sun-dried slices of meat from the hind-quarters of an animal living on an inaccessible island, with a gestation period of twenty-seven months and recently added to the list of endangered species. With our latest offer, he gets all of this bounty for, well, nothing.

Stuck on my fridge at the moment are temptations from almost all of Cambridge's eateries – £10 off the bill, all food half-price, one person in four eats free. Every evening I say to myself, well, I could make a nutritious and balanced meal from salad and falafel, but who am I kidding? The trouble is that these are the deals that just keep on giving: when it comes to my saddlebags, it is indeed, grow one, get one free.

And knickers to you too

8 June 2009

Last night I went to the Mumford Theatre and saw a show called "The Knicker Lady". This doesn't count as free advertising for the show, as it was one night only and the lady in question has already hotfooted it back to her vicarage. That's not a joke: she is married to a chap who has, perhaps inevitably and with thanks to the accepting nature of the C of E when it comes to the foibles of its representatives, become known as the Knicker Vicar. Anyway, the show is a hilarious romp (words usually associated with hammy productions involving under-stair cupboards and knowing winks, but – in this case – entirely true) through the history of the undergarment. The opportunities for pun are legion: it's a brief tale of the seamless progression of the foundation of our obsession with knickers (and bras and girdles and suspenders and even a rather alarming early pair of men's Y-no-fronts with a gaping hole where one might reasonably expect some coverage).

In common with much of the audience, I should imagine (and the audience was mostly female, with the notable exception of the chap sitting alone in the front row and calling out "Bravo!" and "Well done!" after particularly amusing episodes), I went home and cast a critical eye over my own drawer of drawers. It seems that when it comes to intimate apparel, I am a woman of catholic, one might almost say monastic (what is the female equivalent of monastic? nunnish?), tastes: 95% of my smalls are black or white. (Not black *and* white –

who wants to strip down and look like an Everton mint? Except perhaps the Newcastle United WAGs. Or the Everton ones. What? They wear blue? What a confusing game.)

I do occasionally succumb to "Fantasy Susan". This is not anything mucky, before you start writing in for signed photos. This is the Susan I think I should be: she glides effortlessly through her work, achieving world-renown in many fields (hah!), before returning to her pristine home (double hah!), preparing a delicious and nutritious meal with no trace of chocolate (more hahs than can be counted) and then reclining in her window-seat to listen to opera (that's –era, not –rah). Throughout this, she is dressed in classic, elegant yet flattering clothes, underpinned with silky, frothy nothings that (a) match, (b) require a second mortgage, and (c) don't come in a zip-lock bag from M&S.

Nighty-night

21 September 2009

I live in a small terraced house. A very wealthy friend once came to visit, and her five-year old daughter looked around and exclaimed, "Mummy! It's just like Katya's room!" Katya is their au pair, so patently I'm in the wrong job. One of the features of our bijou residence is a staircase with a very tight turn: let's just say that if we ever need a stair-lift fitted, it will be more like coming down a fireman's pole. So it was somewhat of an oversight to forget this when we went into a bed shop a few weeks ago and were seduced by the snoozy music and soft lighting into deciding to upgrade to a king-size bed. (Mind you, after traipsing around the shops all day, a quick lie-down on a park bench would have seemed idyllic – and a sight cheaper.) We've managed perfectly well with a double for decades, but these bed shops know what they're about: what man can resist the offer of an extra six inches?

Getting the bed itself upstairs was no problem – it arrived in sixty-eight small pieces with no assembly instructions. The help-line said that this was because it was self-explanatory, which is oddly enough not the word my poor husband used after three hours with the Allen keys and (more alarmingly) the jigsaw.

The mattress was another matter entirely. The delivery men tried to help, which is an offer they came to regret as they found themselves wedged, seemingly for life, in our stairwell. The horror of their situation struck home when a mobile rang and one of them said, with true terror in his voice, "I can't reach me phone!" I doubt he'd ever been out of contact with "hedoffice" before. They pushed from below, my husband heaved from above, and the cat and I hovered in the hallway calling out helpful instructions along the lines of "Oooh, mind that light!" and "White with two sugars, everyone?".

After forty minutes, I witnessed an historic event: three men agreed that they were beaten. They had been bested by a lump of latex. The delivery men filtered themselves through the banisters, the mattress went back into the van, the bed was dismantled into its sixty-eight component pieces, and the double bed was reinstated. Just for a laugh, I'm thinking of suggesting getting a water-bed. I bet Katya's got a king-size one.

Retail recall

18 October 2010

Now I like a bargain handbag as much as the next woman – and probably more than some – so I'm quite happy to see "discount retailer" TK Maxx in our flagship store on Market Street. (And I use the description with all accuracy: have you noticed how the front of the shop is just like the prow of a ship?) But its arrival does make me feel old – and not because all of their party frocks are cut at least a foot higher at the hem and six inches lower at the neck than I would wear these days. No: it's because I can remember not only the previous tenants of that shop, but also the one before them. You know you've lived in a town for a long time when that happens.

When I first arrived in Cambridge, we had three – yes, children, three – department stores. Where TK Maxx now resides we had the marvellous Eaden Lilley, with a wonderful basement cookware department, and on Monsoon's corner there was Joshua Taylor (not the man – the shop). Talking of men on corners, who remembers the gentlemen's outfitters on the corner of Sidney Street and Green Street, the splendidly named Bodger's the Man's Shop? I pooh-poohed it in my ignorant youth, but now I would give almost anything to be able to present male relatives at Christmas with gift garments labelled "Bodger".

Sliding smoothly on to the topic of labels, one of my most sorely missed shops is the Heffers stationery store, which spread over four floors in what is now Black's. Four floors of stationery: I go weak at the knees just thinking about it. Frankly, a few Cambridge-themed notebooks and the odd calendar in Blackwells do not cut the mustard for this papyrophile (made up word, but you get it).

And with mustard in mind (I'm on fire today with my connections), I pause for a moment to lament the passing of Angeline's Restaurant (now B Bar). When my father visited me at university, he – in the manner of all visiting parents – was dragooned into taking me out to eat. He did it gladly, with the proviso that all meals had to be partaken at Angeline's. We once ate there eleven times in a row – and every meal was perfect. Angeline even catered our wedding, giving in to my pleas for a three-tier chocolate cake with only the faintest lift of her Gallic eyebrows. Now that was an entente cordiale.

Food chains

13 December 2010

A French friend recently asked about our supermarkets. I thought she was going to flaunt her patisseries and fromageries in my face, but she actually wanted to learn about the ranking of our supermarkets; where do the rich people shop, she wanted to know. I mentioned Harrods and Fortnum's – and their white truffle rissoles steeped in caviar and the like – but she meant ordinarily rich rather than unimaginably rich. And I realised that we Brits know this instinctively – so much for us being a classless society.

At the top of the tree is Waitrose, with its soft lighting and wide aisles. They offer a most dangerous innovation: you swipe your credit card to get a magic gun to read the barcodes as you fill your trolley with edible frou-frous, and it's not like spending real money at all. As I have the self-control of a half-starved Rottweiler, I allow myself only rare visits. A more frequent treat is M&S, although I rather think it's gone downhill since it started selling things not made personally by St Michael and stacking the special offer biscuits in cardboard boxes. My regular haunt comes next in the pecking order: the orange wonder that is Sainsbury's. If you ignore their constant blandishments to try something new today (like Waitrose, perhaps) and their inexplicable yet enduring love affair with pukka Jamie, they're a good solid supermarket.

Next is the chain that I think must be Britain's most popular, given the number of outlets they have – Tesco. Because I'm a contrary sort of person, this very ubiquity is what chased me away – I think they're planning to take over the world, and frankly I'm a bit scared of them. Within four miles of my central Cambridge larder, for instance, there are nine Tescos (Tescoses? Tesci?).

Then we have Asda, of which I am rather fond because they employ older people and you can always have a nice little chat at the tills. I think Morrison's comes next – although I've never been to the Cambourne one, which may be decorated with original artworks and have maths PhD students on the tills, so I apologise if I have mis-ranked. And bringing up the rear are ALDI and Lidl – according to Wikipedia, the latter chain has "about 9,001 stores worldwide". So not "about 9,000", then? My French friend listened politely, shook her head at my class obsession, and headed to her local independent butcher.

A good fit

24 January 2011

There are few things more mortifying than being stuck in a changing room. I don't mean wedged into the cubicle – although that must be a tad embarrassing – but rather imprisoned inside an item of clothing with no visible means of escape.

I dashed into Laura Ashley one lunchtime last week and spotted a likely dress on a size 12 hanger. Trying on clothes in the winter is a trial at the best of times, what with nineteen layers to peel off, and so I failed to notice that the dress itself was a size 10. It slipped on easily enough, the cunning devil, but of course would not zip up. Or come off. Or budge in any direction at all, once I had pulled the skirt over my head and was now stranded waving my arms like a particularly lumpy jelly-fish in opaque tights. I pulled, I heaved, I held my breath before remembering that this actually makes you bigger (and a bit dizzy).

I heard a salesgirl outside and considered calling for help, but what with everyone having camera-phones these days, I couldn't risk appearing on a website called whatwereyouthinkinglumpybum.com. I tried to think rationally, and reasoned that come closing time (a mere five hours away), the store would clear and surely someone would check the changing rooms… After a few minutes (perhaps I had lost an ounce or two through panic), I managed to wiggle one shoulder free, and it was plain sailing from there.

I'm not a posh shop shopper (I have an aversion to transparently thin sale staff who call you "moddom"), but I do like their changing rooms. Some of them are considerably nicer than my lounge, and I would happily move in – although I am not sure that they would be as keen to see my world-beating collection of cushions and "Dallas" DVDs. The transparent ones glide around behind you, relieving you of the debilitating weight of some expensive frou-frou or other, to put in moddom's changing room. I daresay that they have subtle call buttons for jelly-fish emergencies.

The other thing that bothers me about changing rooms is that everyone else's choices always seem better. As I jelly-fished in Laura Ashley, I heard someone say, "Oh, that top is fantastic on you – great colour, goes with everything, and such a bargain!". Only my constrained posture kept me from bursting through the curtain shouting "Gimme gimme!". As I said, mortifying.

Another north/south divide

6 August 2012

I have an O level in economics, you know. It's a source of much amusement to my husband, who enjoys watching my head implode as I try to figure out whether 33% more detergent is a better deal than 33% off the price of the bottle (it isn't, apparently – who knew?). But I mention it so that you know that I have some qualification, albeit dating from 1982, for what I am about to say. And I want you to cut out this column and store it somewhere safe, so that when what I predict comes to pass, I can prove that I was right, and moreover, that I said it before either Robert Peston or Nick Robinson.

You know we're having a bit of trouble with the euro? It turns out – and who could have foreseen this – that inviting everyone you know to join your currency club, and promising to provide them with financial support no matter what, is not actually terribly practical. People will, despite all PC efforts, continue in general to conform to their national stereotypes. The Germans will work very hard and make good quality items that other people want to buy. The Italians will promise to try harder, and indeed the ones living up north near the Germans will do just that – but the ones in the hot south, where there is pasta to be cooked and sun to be soaked up, will just have a nice gelato and worry about it later. And the Greeks, it seems, are unfortunately blessed with finance ministers who did their O levels even longer ago than I did.

So I have come up with a solution. Rather than getting rid of the euro entirely (which I understand might cause something of a kerfuffle, financially speaking), why don't we split it into two? A northern currency and a southern one would give us the benefits of "monetary union" (whatever that may be) while allowing countries to join either the Jets or the Sharks, so to speak. And we can also get rid of the name "euro" – which sounds like a name that a nerdy games designer might come up with, after discarding "moon dollar" and "buckaroo". The northern currency should be the florin – lots of history, sounds solid. And the southern currency can be the siesta – sounds southern, easy to say, and designed to stop you doing daft things in the heat of the moment.

Trolley couture

9 September 2013

We regularly go on holiday to Switzerland (what better destination for a train-loving chocoholic married to a man who dreams of cycling up mountains?) and nearly always choose self-catering accommodation. Call me daft (I heard that), but I love foreign supermarkets – I like to see what's popular, and how it's packaged, and what's familiar and what isn't. (The Swiss, for instance, aren't keen on biscuits and completely lack "le gateau de Jaffa", but their cheese counter is a symphony in dairy.)

And when I go shopping en Suisse I have noticed that the shopping trolley is de rigueur. I don't mean the malevolent, squeaky, metal thing you battle with in the supermarket, but rather the elegant, streamlined one you take to and from the place with your purchases. Here in England they have remained rather the province of the proverbial little old lady, but in Switzerland everyone – regardless of gender and age – has a natty little trolley.

And boy do I mean natty. We were walking through a very upmarket shopping street in Lausanne, and passed a luggage boutique. One window was showcasing their latest handbags, balanced on mock columns and with eye-watering price-tags. The other window had a fantastic display of – yes – shopping trolleys, arranged on a race-track with a large poster of Monaco as the back-drop, to stress their speed and desirability. None of your tatty tartan here; there was one trolley in virginal white with a simple gold clasp to the lid, another in a witty cow print, a third in traditional wicker, and one with trendy Missoni stripes. Tempted? I should say I was. But something held me back.

Reader, you know that I am not particularly vain. I gave up following fashion years ago, when I realised that it led to some very odd places, and I actually prefer finding second-hand dresses on eBay that are exactly the same as the ones I have worn and loved for years. But I do worry that here in Cambridge a shopping trolley – even one with a cow print – might not have quite the cachet that it does in Lausanne. (Mind you, dragging home six cartons of juice and a four-pinter of milk and ending up with a stoop and baboon arms is not a good look either.) What we need is a critical mass, so if you have a trolley yourself, stand up straight and roll with pride.

The battle of the bulge

2 February 2015

Last weekend I went to a birthday party, for a friend who is significantly older than I am (well, thirteen months…) and who wanted to celebrate her fiftieth in style. So off we toddled to a country house hotel for fizz and dancing – and a black tie dress code.

In December my husband strapped on his head-torch and delved into the unexplored reaches of our loft to unearth his dinner jacket; it fitted reasonably well then, and rather more snugly after Christmas, but it would do. With advance warning I had bought myself a little black dress in the July sales, but decided to leave the underpinning for later consideration. Yes, ladies: you know whereof I speak if I say the phrase "magic knickers". And my first three weeks of this new year were spent not in contemplation of life's big questions (why are we here? have I achieved my life's goals? what sort of abomination is the chocolate Pop-Tart?) but rather in search of an undergarment that would meet several conflicting criteria.

First and foremost, it had to make me look good to the outside world, with curves going in and out at the right places and in the right proportions. Second, I had to be able to get into and out of it – not with any degree of elegance particularly, but at all. And third, I had to be able to breathe, sit, dine and dance in it. The last time I sought such a garment was many years ago, and on reflection, what was I thinking? Back then my natural figure was perfectly fine – but such is the self-consciousness of youth.

And clothing technology has certainly moved on. You can now get not only magic knickers, but also magic shorts, thongs, body stockings, full body cases (with or without built-in bra) and almost any other permutation, and in an endless variety of fabrics with differing degrees of elasticity. I tried on dozens of the things, bringing an unappealing flush to my face and other regions. But still the undeniable fact remains: if you squish out fat from one place, it has to go somewhere. So you end up with a peculiar underarm sausage, or boobs you can't see over, or very pudgy knees. Eventually I decided instead on diversionary tactics, and danced so wildly and with such lack of co-ordination and shame that no-one even noticed my misplaced bulges.

3 TRANSPORT

On the buses

12 March 2007

This week I had to go to the sports injuries clinic at Addenbrooke's.   No, I haven't let you down and become all sporty – let's just say that I had an embarrassing incident involving a dangerously high-heeled pair of boots and a kerbstone, but as my knee was twisted, I prepared a moving story about an amazing, match-winning final drop-shot in the county squash championships and set off for the clinic.

Never one to bear pain stoically, I soon found that I could neither push down the accelerator pedal in the car without crying, nor face the prospect of a long, wet bike ride to the hospital. I know, I thought with naïve optimism, I'll take the bus: there's a stop near my house and I'm sure there must be a suitable route. I hobbled pitifully to the bus stop – I knew it was a bus stop because the big metal sign said "Bus Stop" and the lettering in the road said (you're ahead of me here) "Bus Stop". A bus approached, I waved my arm, and the bus did not stop. Lying sign. Lying road. It was in fact a "Bus Go" that I was standing at. After three hours and four more buses (I may be exaggerating here – it was nowhere near that number of buses) a kind pensioner explained to me that this bus stop is no longer used and that I should walk further up the road to the new one. "Why is the sign still here? And the road markings?" I asked. She smiled pityingly.

I waited another four months at the other stop, and finally a bus deigned to pull up. I almost married the driver, so grateful was I to see him. The feeling was not mutual – he barely acknowledged me and cunningly waited until I was halfway down the aisle before roaring off at Mach 3. I apologised to the man in whose lap I was now sitting, and then settled back to enjoy the journey. It was a circuitous route, to say the least. We went through villages I had never heard of, and some where the locals turned out in force to see the new-fangled horseless buggy rush past. The distant sighting of the Angel of the North was also a surprise. Eventually, sometime after dusk, we drew up at Addenbrooke's; the other passengers and I were such firm friends by then that we exchanged addresses and promised to keep in touch and have an annual reunion. But perhaps there is method in the madness: I had been sitting still for so long – precisely the medical advice they give for knee injuries – that all was well and I had no need of the clinic after all. And I was able to walk home – a journey that took only three hours, much shorter than the bus journey there.

Parking for beginners

28 May 2007

Before I start, let me set the scene. In my household we have two adults, no children, one cat and one car. Oh, and thirteen bicycles. My husband was a rabid cyclist when I met him back in the dark ages (must have been the initial excitement following the invention of the wheel) and in a shameful attempt to get him to notice me, I pretended to give a hoot about matters cycling. My cover as a competent cyclist was blown when I catapulted over the handlebars on our first date, but perhaps he felt it would be ungentlemanly to laugh like a drain and then dump me. Unless you're live on "Big Brother", of course.

So for me, parking in Cambridge is mainly a spectator sport. And for sheer entertainment value, it beats WWF wrestling, spoilt tennis players having hissy fits and even Prince Philip being thrown out of a carriage by a pair of staunchly republican horses.

There's the synchronised dash, best observed outside Homebase on a Saturday afternoon, when two drivers at opposite ends of the car park spot the same space at the same time. Casting No Entry signs and directional arrows to the wind, they speed to the location, winding down their windows to yell the battle-cry "But I was here first!".

Then there's the parallel freestyle, best viewed on the Backs. Having confirmed that he has not chosen a space reserved for coaches, ice-cream vans, film crews or boat trailers, the driver screeches to a halt – extra points being awarded if he can make the traffic back up beyond the mini-roundabout. He then realises that, despite his full quota of testosterone, he is in fact unable to parallel park and spends twenty minutes jiggling ineffectively backwards and forwards in the space, nudging a nanometre closer to the kerb with each movement. Meanwhile, his wife and kids have been set to busking, to earn the king's ransom in coins needed to feed the ravenous meter.

And finally there's the King's Parade relay event, where a minimum of forty cars an hour must cruise up KP in disbelief, spoiling the view and polluting the air, ignoring the dead end signs and reasoning that the restriction must apply to everyone else. Extra points are awarded for the neatness of the twenty-seven point turn outside Great St Mary's, while points are deducted for each cyclist, tourist or itinerant opera singer mown down in the process. Automatic disqualification will follow the massacre of an entire graduation crocodile.

Giving roundabouts the runabout

10 September 2007

You have no idea how lucky you are that I am here to write this column this week. (Mind you, I daresay it depends on your viewpoint: perhaps some of you have been fashioning images of me in wax and are now muttering darkly under your breath and breaking open a new box of sharp pins.) But the real point is that I have had a Narrow Escape.

There I was, cycling happily around daffodil roundabout (do keep up – the one where Jesus Lane meets Victoria Avenue) when the bus in front of me flung out the anchors and came to a juddering halt. My bike brakes and I squealed in unison, and we stopped dead about a nanometre (or whatever is the smallest perceptible distance – slightly greater than that between Tony Blair's lips and George Bush's bottom, let's say) from the bus's rear end. (Goodness, that Blair/Bush analogy was more realistic than I had thought.)

So what had happened? Had a pedestrian stepped out in front of perhaps the only bus driver in Cambridge who would actually stop in such an instance? Had a little bunny-wunny hopped onto the road? Had a rising bollard been moved by those waggish students? No, no and no. In fact, the bus driver had spotted another bus waiting to come onto the roundabout and had stopped to let him on. Let me say that again: STOPPED TO LET HIM ON.

Now I'm no professional driver; I will admit to girlish panics when I stall at the traffic lights, but will then counter that by revealing that I am an absolute whiz at parallel parking. And I do know that once you are on a roundabout, you have right of way and you continue going because those behind you will expect it of you and if you stop they will end up impaled on your exhaust pipe.

But I'm open to new ideas, so here's my suggestion: if bus drivers can do it, so can the rest of us. Perhaps the fairest arrangement is to group road users by type and then by colour. So if you drive a red car, feel free to allow other red cars onto the roundabout in front of you. (To assist red/green colour-blind drivers, please paint a big R on your bonnet.) I as a cyclist shall regally wave on great gangs of other cyclists – particularly if they are foreign language students and intend to go the wrong way round the roundabout. And if you drive a white van, well, you'll do whatever you like anyway.

Barriers to sanity

11 February 2008

I'm a big fan of "Brief Encounter". Remember the speck of grit in the eye, the endless joyless cups of tea, the self-sacrificing Laura sending stoic Dr Alec off to "Ifrica" with only a slight mutual wobble in the RP? However, I see that First Network One Great Eastern or whatever they are called this week have done their bit to discourage adulterous eye-care by installing ticket barriers at Cambridge station. This is the station that is slated for total remodelling soon, so I can only assume that the barriers will rise again, noble and phoenix-like, from the rubble.

One unexpected development is that, unless you have a ticket for travel, you can no longer get onto the platform, so it's farewell to those fond farewells. I asked the phalanx of guards now positioned to help people whose tickets get wedged in the slots or whose bodies get wedged in the barriers what can be done about this. Can one buy a tuppenny platform ticket from a machine on the wall? Alas no – because if you go onto the platform without a travel ticket, you are not insured.

As the guard told me this, we were watching an elderly lady and her shopping trolley being eaten alive by a rather zealous barrier, which had slammed shut as she was halfway through. Two other guards wrestled to free her, to the accompaniment of osteoporosis-riddled limbs snapping like twigs under the impact. "She'll be

OK, you see, because she's insured," said my guard smugly. A great comfort to her, I am sure.

Another reason for the change is apparently (all together now) the threat of terrorism. It seems that a suicide bomber who has spent two years training hard at some bleak camp in rural Afghanistan is going to abort his mission to blow up the 0745 to King's Cross when he finds he can't get on the platform without buying a £1.20 single to Waterbeach. Our only hope is that his bomb-laden rucksack gets stuck in the new barriers.

Watlingon Ho!

5 May 2008

There are many advantages to living in Cambridge. It is a breathtakingly beautiful city, stuffed to the gills with history and drama. When you travel abroad, people have always heard of it. And it's not Oxford. So perhaps it is to redress the balance of fairness that First Capital Connect has decided to levy a Cambridge Surcharge on its train tickets. I was on the train this morning, having paid £36 and a share in my kidney for the delights of travelling on a one-day peak Travelcard. When the Revenue Maximisation Operative (né ticket inspector) came past, the nice chap sitting opposite me asked him for a one-day peak Travelcard from Watlington and was charged £32.

My geography is rather hazy, but isn't Watlington waaaay further north than Cambridge? Further from London? More miles for less money? I asked the RMO why I had paid more. "Because you're Cambridge," he explained, as though to a particularly daft spaniel. After many minutes of me reverting to petulant toddler-hood and answering his every sentence with "But why?", we finally determined that if you live in Watlington, you can get a cheaper Travelcard at any time, and moreover you are not banned from the highly sought-after trains that leave King's Cross at the times you might actually want to come home. But if you're from Cambridge, you have to hang around KX with the tramps and the ladies of dubious virtue until late evening.

By now my ever-louder bewilderment had caught the attention of most of the carriage. The Watlingtonians were looking smug – until someone else ruined their fun by revealing that he was in fact travelling on an even-cheaper ticket from Watlington to Epsom because a kindly RMO had once told him it was the cheapest possible way to get to London. He wasn't even sure where Epsom was, but it saved him four quid a day so he felt very warmly towards the place. The Cantabrigians were muttering and tutting. The RMO scarpered into First Class and hid behind a portly gentleman.

So I now have two options. I could move to Watlington, thus requiring this column to be renamed "Susan in the Sticks". Or I could buy a return ticket to Watlington and on the way home pretend to come over all peculiar and have to get off the train for a breath of fresh air in, oh, Cambridge.

Twenty's plenty, but thirty's dirty

2 June 2008

A couple of weekends ago, before the onset of the recent Biblical storms and floods, my husband and I went out on our tandem. Sneakily, despite my best efforts at map-reading around it, he managed to steer us to the foot of Chapel Hill in Haslingfield. As any serious Cambridge cyclist knows, this is our Everest, our Kilimanjaro, our Snowden – The Only Hill for Miles. We slogged, we puffed, we complained (that's the royal we), and finally crested the summit before freewheeling down into Barrington. Eyes streaming, I clung on for dear life, cheeks (all four of them) wobbling madly. "How fast are we going?" I gasped. "Just over thirty," he confirmed. I can tell you, thirty feels blooming fast when all that lies between flesh and tarmac is a rather fetching sky-blue pair of padded shorts.

All of this is a long introduction to my latest obsession: people driving too fast in town. My dear departed granddad was possibly the worst driver this country has ever produced – one of the generation who didn't bother with niceties like a licence, but simply hopped into a car and gave it a go. Thankfully his finances limited him to a motorbike and sidecar and then – in the heady sixties – to a zippy red Mini. His proud boast was that he had never had an accident – but his erratic driving style certainly caused plenty, which he would have spotted had he ever looked into his rear-view mirror. But even he respected the speed limits, with his mantra "it's a limit, not a target". I know that thirty can feel slow when you come off the M11, but the pedestrians you whistle past feel as though their eyebrows are being peeled off.

I'm worried that Cambridge is becoming too car-centric. One of my regular crossing points, on Fen Causeway, has had the pedestrian lights adjusted so that I can virtually knit myself a Volvo in the time it takes for them to stop the traffic. Surely fresh people, out and about under their own steam, should have priority over the tinned variety? It's worse in the rain, as you stand there dripping by the side of the road while smug dry drivers swish past and flip puddles over your head.

Cambridge is a higgledy-piggledy place, with narrow, winding roads, skinny bridges, skinnier pavements and uneven cobbles – and we love it. Please don't let the car take over and herd the pedestrians into terrified crowds on islands – or we'll turn into Oxford.

You've got to hand it to the airlines

13 October 2008

Thanks to the miracle of modern technology, I am writing this while waiting for a flight at Stansted Airport. Regular readers will know my views on current security checks, and the associated joy of stripping down to your smalls while experts zap your bag with x-rays and raise their eyebrows suggestively at each other. It's an extendable laser pointer for presentations, in case you're wondering.

However, not content with forcing us to disrobe in public and suggesting that we cannot be trusted with more than three drops of liquid, airlines are now imposing charges for services that – foolish optimist that I am – I had thought were an integral part of the flying experience. Like checking in. And taking a suitcase. Imagine if garages charged one price per litre of petrol, and then added a surcharge if you wanted to use a pump and hose to collect it.

But it seems that the travelling worm is turning. You can avoid both the check-in charge and the unreasonable-desire-to-take-clothes-with-you charge if you carry hand luggage only and check in online before you leave home. (As the check in procedure was originally intended to confirm that you had made it to the airport and were ready to fly, and to give the ground staff an opportunity to look you in the eye and weed out the raving loons and the drunks, I find the concept of checking in at home a bit freaky, but if you can marry a chap you've only met online, why not?) So people are becoming adept at stuffing more and more into their hand luggage. Some airlines now let you take any weight "within reason". On a recent flight, I saw a little old lady sweetly ask the burly chap next to her to help her put her wheelie case in the overhead bin, and I fear the poor lad's rugby career (if not his intimate relations) will suffer for months. He tried to look nonchalant, but the popping veins told their own story.

And as you're allowed to take on board everything you've bought in the duty free zone, why not travel really light? Come through security with just your boarding card and passport tucked into your undies, and then buy everything "airside". Depending on which airport you're using, you could end up with some unusual outfits, but who knows – you might find that lederhosen or kilts are really you.

Going deep under cover

27 April 2009

I recently renewed my car insurance (I know what you're thinking: I bet Jane Austen wishes she'd started "Pride and Prejudice" with a humdinger of a line like that, instead of all that twaddle about rich single men, although for her it would have been carriage insurance). And I discovered two things (apart from a deep and abiding affection for Aleksandr the meerkat, of course).

First, I have about four centuries of no claims discount accruing to me. Incredible though it sounds, since I bought my beloved car in 1987 (that's not a typo: my little blue machine and I have been cruising the mean streets together for over twenty years) I have never made a claim on my insurance. Not once. Nada. Zip. I am the dream client for these companies: not only is the car approaching vintage status, but so is the driver. When I organised the renewal, the nice chap on the phone was going patiently through his questionnaire and asked, "Will you be using the vehicle in off-road or performance racing events?" We both cried with laughter. The closest I get to off-road is pulling into a nice layby for a sandwich.

And second, I found that I have insured the same car twice. For the same year. There is such a thing as too much coverage – although not a concept likely to trouble Jordan and Peter André any time soon. I am usually a rather hyper-organised person, so I can't imagine what went wrong. In the car insurance folder there are two sections, neatly labelled "Insurance 1" and "Insurance 2", so it must have made sense at some point – no doubt I was choc-deprived at the time.

But what I over-insure in one department, I under-insure in another. (Any insurance reps reading this, don't even bother: better men have tried and failed.) I'm a big fan of the NHS and can't justify private health insurance just to get slightly nicer wallpaper, a potted palm and Bourbon creams for visitors. And as for employment insurance, if my work dries up I'm planning to live off my husband. He doesn't know this yet, so let's not mention it. But if anyone knows of a "dependent spouse with expensive shoe, magazine and chocolate habit to support" policy, do send him the bumf. He might even take it out twice – or would that be bigaminsurance?

Just within Reach

16 May 2009

What is it about the words "Bank Holiday Monday" that makes the sun take fright and the wind swing around to the perishing direction? And so it was that I found myself shivering outside the Fort St George last Monday morning, waiting to set off with a group of hardy souls on the annual bike ride to Reach Fair. Despite having lived in Cambridge since 1984, I had never been to this fair, which has taken place every year since 1201 – I believe Terry Wogan ran a promo for the first one on his Radio 2 breakfast show.

Incurable optimist that I am, I spent most of the ride pointing out miniscule patches of blue sky and chirruping, "It's only a quick shower – just blowing over!" When I arrived at Reach, my hands had frozen on the handlebars, so we tottered over to the tea tent for a reviving brew. And I was delighted to see that it was a proper tea tent, with WI-ish ladies overseeing giant urns and having hissed disagreements along the lines of "But Marjorie, you know very well that I always do the ginger sponge – the Swiss roll is your department. I've never been beyond Boulogne, on that day-trip with the Brownies, so what do I know about alpine baking?"

At noon the Mayor of Cambridge opened the fair with the traditional wording, warning all who caused trouble or cheated the public that there would be hell to pay. I did give a hard stare to the chap who had charged me £1.50 for a cone containing about four chips, but he seemed disinclined to turn himself in to the aldermen. (Talking of aldermen, this year's mayor was accompanied by an all-female troupe of alderpeople, which gave him the air of a mediaeval Hugh Hefner parading around the fair.) I very much enjoyed watching him (the mayor, not Hugh) riding the wooden swing-boats (and no, that's not an obscure euphemism – although I like the sound of it and may start using it with a knowing wink) with a chap dressed as a judge – it was like falling into a scene from Monty Python.

Talking of euphemisms, we have a friend who will often comment, "He's the sort of chap who hangs his curtains in the Dutch fashion, if you know what I mean". We've never dared say that no, we don't. Printable suggestions on a postcard, please.

School run, walk, drive and cycle

22 November 2010

When I went to school, sometime in the early nineteenth century, education was seen as a privilege. I woke up before dawn, rinsed my uniform in a freezing stream and spit-polished my shoes, then fed the chickens before walking four miles to school. At the weekends, I sang for sailors in order to make the money to buy textbooks. OK, all of that is complete tosh – except the bit about the sailors – but despite my cushy childhood, what I did not have was a parental lift to school every day. No: although I went to a posh expat school in the tropics, where chauffeur-driven Mercedes were de rigueur, of the 1,200 of us at the school, precisely nine were driven to school each day. The rest of us took advantage of three amazing innovations: the leg (best in pairs), the bicycle and above all the school bus.

I was reminded of this today, as I cycled along Trumpington Street at about 8am. It was nose-to-tail school runners, with the largest cars (slightly smaller than a tank) containing the smallest children (slightly larger than a squirrel in plaits). We spend endless time and money trying to tempt our children off their ever-increasing backsides and out into the fresh air for exercise, and here is a golden opportunity being missed. The most prevalent reason that parents give for not allowing their children to walk or cycle to school is that there is too much traffic – which (and surely this is obvious to all) they themselves are creating. And it seems that the safety of other people's children is of no concern at all, judging by the number of cars double-parked, driven up onto the kerb, halted on the zig-zag lines and performing numerous other infringements.

Harking back to my own experience, the bus trip to and from school was a highlight of the day. I travelled with my best friend, and we had all the important discussions: who fancied whom, how long they had fancied them for, why they fancied them rather than us, and what we were going to wear to the next disco. It taught me punctuality (time and bus driver wait for no child), negotiation skills (for nabbing the back row from bigger kids) and road sense (cross behind the bus not in front of it – time and bus driver, etc.). I wouldn't have traded it for a dull parental lift to school at any price.

Nannying on the rails

7 February 2011

I'm not keen on the term "nanny state", as I think it gives nannies a bad name. Mary Poppins is a marvellous character, and anyone who can listen to Dick Van Dyke's tortured accent for several scenes without braining him with her umbrella deserves our respect. But I began to see the accuracy of the term when I travelled down to London the other day on a train provided by First Capital Great Eastern West Anglia – or whatever our local company is called this week.

As I boarded, I was warned by the driver on the intercom to sit down and hold on as we were about to couple – well, not he and I, but our train and one lately arrived from the Fens. The way he talked, you'd think it was going to be like the clashing of stag antlers at rutting time, with passengers clinging on for dear life, rather than the gentle whispering bump we actually experienced.

After that trauma we were all congratulating each other on surviving and calling family members to reassure them, when a well-spoken recorded lady said that she would like to give us some information to help us "board and alight safely". Thank goodness, as I had been worrying about this aspect of my journey, what with stepping up and down being a new concept. "Do not attempt to enter or leave the train while the hustle alarm is sounding," she warned. Does she not realise than in London no-one even starts to think about considering maybe boarding until they hear the "hustle alarm" – that's beeps, to you and me.

I had only just finished taking careful notes of these instructions when she came back to explain that seats are for people, and all luggage should be stowed on the overhead racks. But what about shoulder injuries from lifting? What if my scarf falls off the rack and entwines itself around a sleeping commuter's neck? I feel we need guidance. And when we finally completed our hazardous journey, pale with anxiety, she kindly reminded us to take all our belongings with us. Infuriating, as I had been planning to lighten the load by leaving my handbag to go up and down the east coast line a few times while I was at work.

How soon before trains are festooned with signs saying: "Beware! High-speed transport! Moves on rails!"? It's a train, for heaven's sake – not the space shuttle.

Airports wars

17 December 2012

When God designed hell, he almost certainly modelled it on Heathrow: alongside the busiest motorway in the country (so every journey requires a six-hour contingency in case of jams), with numerous terminals (making it highly likely that you will go to the wrong one), all with claustrophobically low ceilings and jaundice-inducing yellow lighting. Heaven, on the other hand, is where you end up if London City Airport is full – which it never is. What a joy: there are always more seats than passengers, and free wifi everywhere.

When I first started using it, Stansted was more LCY than LHR. I used to boast to Londoners that we East Anglians did not have to suffer the twin torments of Heathrow and Gatwick because we were so well served by Stansted. Let me take you back [wavy lines and tinkling bells, please].... Stansted's high ceiling, its sail-like lining designed to minimise sound, allowed light to stream in to the refreshingly empty concourse. A few flights an hour passed noiselessly through the system – for once upon a time, you know, Stansted was a tannoy-free airport, with flight updates on screens only. You could drop off your loved ones just outside the terminal, so that they could walk under cover into the building, and after a quick jaunt through security they would head off into the clouds.

Back to today [wavy lines,etc.].... The ceiling is still high, but every available inch of floor space both landside and airside has been crammed with retail opportunities. The smell of clashing cuisines fills the place, against a background soundtrack of those racing car games in the arcade. To get the message across over the cacophony, repeated announcements are made about it being the "very last and final call for the three remaining passengers to somewhere ghastly". The security queues stretch almost to Audley End, and quite how far down you need to strip seems to depend on the mood/masochism level of the person manning the conveyor belt. And worst of all, they have just introduced a fee for dropping off at the terminal: £2 for a ten-minute "express drop-off". Otherwise, it's a free drop-off in the mid-stay car-park, and a ten-minute bus journey to the terminal. Stansted has lost sight of the purpose of the airport – i.e. to serve passengers. At London City, you drive right up to the terminal – and a man in a top hat opens your door. Sheer heaven, I tell you.

Big buses

11 February 2013

I'm very fond of buses. I once lived a whole year with a grandmother who viewed them as mobile community centres, and would quite happily go miles past our stop "because we were having a nice chat". For the most part, buses are painted in cheery colours, you get an unbeatable view from the upper deck, and on cold days their steamed-up windows and diffused lighting look very snug. But here in Cambridge I rarely use them as a passenger, and instead interact with them mainly from outside. And from outside, they are really, really scary.

I think it's mainly a matter of proportions: Cambridge buses are far too big for Cambridge. Our streets were built for horses, and then expanded slightly to allow those tall, thin Ford Populars to pass each other in a polite 1950s manner. What they were not designed to accommodate are the gargantuan double decker buses that loom and sway their way around town nowadays.

There are plenty of hairy corners I could name, but perhaps the worst is where Jesus Lane turns (physically and by name) into Bridge Street – there's a posh patisserie on the corner, usually with dribble marks on the windows. If you're walking on the outside of that bend when a bus running late comes along, look out for those wing mirrors at head height – they pack quite a punch. Bridge Street itself is not much better; at peak hours, with buses stopping on both sides of the street, it takes a slimmer cyclist than I to filter herself between them. (Not that I'm fat –I've just got big panniers.)

Why, I wonder, can't we have two sizes of bus: the monsters for rush hour, when we need to shift lots of people, and then little shuttles for the other times. Somehow I mind less about waiting behind a full bus than being held up by a 12 ton metal box transporting a driver and two passengers. My husband pointed out that this would mean big buses sitting idle for most of the day, but I've had an idea: can't they be used for day trips for pensioners or school children, or anyone who wants a fun day out? It would bring extra money to the bus company, get their logo out and about, and free up the city centre streets for nippy shuttle buses. Next week: my simple solution to the Arab-Israeli problem.

Endangered animals of all stripes

19 August 2013

Despite the homogenisation of the world, most things are done to perfection in one country and in poorer imitation in others. For ice-cream, it's Italy – we all try, but gelato is king. For theme parks, it's America – who else can match their sheer joy and lack of irony? And for zebra crossings, why, it's England of course. In France they're used for target practice, but here they are the height of civilisation, a (Belisha) beacon of road sharing at its best. Or at least they were.

Last week my husband was assaulted – for the second time in three years – on the zebra leading to Jesus Lock bridge. In both cases, drivers took exception to the way that he – the cheek! the gall! – stepped out onto the stripes and made them stop their cars. In both cases, as they catapulted themselves out of their cars and just before biffing him, the drivers asserted that pedestrians have to wait at the edge of the zebra until drivers stop and that he had in effect cut them up.

Please oh please can we have a campaign to highlight this dangerous misconception? Rule 195 of the Highway Code says: "As you approach a zebra crossing look out for pedestrians waiting to cross and be ready to slow down or stop to let them cross – you MUST [their capitals] give way when a pedestrian has moved onto a crossing." Once you've got a toe on the crossing, it's your right of way – you don't have to wait like a penitent at the side of the road. Of course, lots of pedestrians do wait – perhaps also labouring under the same misunderstanding about who has priority, or maybe they're just being cautious – but sometimes the only way to claim the space is to set foot.

There are so few places on our roads where pedestrians can assert themselves that it seems a terrible shame to sacrifice this one. Another place where they have right of way but rarely enjoy it is when walking along a main road and crossing a side road; the drivers coming out of (or indeed turning into) the side road think that the pedestrians should wait for them, but actually it's the other way round (Highway Code Rule 170).

Pedestrians, let's reclaim the crossings! Walk tall across those stripes. After all, no-one wants to see the lovely zebra on the endangered list.

Ticket turmoil

28 October 2013

It usually starts as a rumour on the platform, whispered from the corner of the mouth. "I've heard..." (looking over shoulder for eavesdropping railway staff) "that if you ask for a ticket starting in Waterbeach, and say that you'll be breaking your journey home in Cambridge, while travelling with three children and an assisted hearing dog, you can leave King's Cross during" (another glance) "the rush hour!" Cambridge has perhaps one of the highest concentrations of Tefal heads in the world, and yet still you will regularly see grown men weeping at the ticket window as they try to understand the fiendish complexities of train ticket pricing.

For a start, we have two London destinations, each is served by a different railway company – or, as I should imagine they have it in their literature, a rail-based travel experience facilitator. The government claims that having dozens of railway companies creates competition but in reality, of course, each route is awarded to one provider – so if you're in a snit with CrossCountry and would love to take your business elsewhere, you haven't a hope of getting to Stansted by train. What the plethora of companies creates is not competition but chaos, and particularly around ticketing.

I have just looked into the options for a ticket to London tomorrow, and I can buy anytime singles or return, off-peak or super-off-peak, carnets (peak and off-peak) and various flavours of travel-card. Determining when is peak or off takes more brain-power than I can muster – especially as it depends on the particular station and not on the clock – and that is without deciding whether to travel in a group for a discount, or sell my house in order to go first class.

I visit Switzerland quite often, and they have really cracked the train pricing. They charge per kilometre travelled, regardless of time of day. So you don't get that crazy situation (which I have encountered recently) where a return ticket costs 5p more than a single, or, conversely, where it's cheaper to buy two singles than a return. Almost every Swiss citizen buys a railcard each year that gives them 50% off the price of all journeys, so the Swiss railway gets guaranteed income in January while the locals feel that they are not subsidising the travel of foreigners like me, who come to sob wildly on their platforms, clutching beautifully simple tickets and crying "Why oh why can't we do it like this?".

Tours de France

7 July 2014

On my very first visit to my husband's student digs, I was astonished by what I saw in his bed. Innocent young slip of a girl that I was, I had never seen such a thing before. It was a gunmetal grey Cliff Shrubb racing bike with Campag Super Record groupset and Mavic SSC wheels with tubular tyres. It was in his bed because he had built it himself and he loved it more than life. Grudgingly, he moved it so that I could sit down – and frankly, that order of priority has persisted in our relationship to this day. In the spirit of "if you can't beat them…", I at first pretended to, and then genuinely acquired, a love of cycling – both doing it and, more enthusiastically, watching whippety-thin men doing it.

Many – indeed most – of our early holidays together were organised around watching cycle races. We hitchhiked all over England to watch various bits of the now-defunct Milk Race and Wincanton Classic, often cheering on the riders from inside our tent as rain bucketed down on all of us. When we were feeling particularly flush we would buy the cheapest seats on the ferry and sleep in train toilets to make our way to any stage of the Holy Grail of road races: the Tour de France.

We watched it in France, where riders are cheered on by families gathered at the roadside with full meals and plenty of wine. We nearly missed it in a small

Dutch town, when the locals had taken such advantage of the excuse to have a big party that the approach of the peloton (the main group of riders) took everyone by surprise. On a mountain-top in Italy I touched the muscular and luscious bottom of my hero Eros Poli under the pretence of helping him up a steep bit. And in Switzerland, I joined in. Yes, I rode alongside the Tour de France.

I was on a postmistress bike rented from the local railway station, and wearing a summer dress and big straw hat. We realised that there was a farm track running parallel to the road on which the riders would whizz past, and as they approached, I cycled like a madwoman along this track. On the other side of the road, my husband stood, camera ready – and as the peloton streamed past, he clicked a perfect photo of a hundred elite athletes in Lycra and one grinning fool in Boden.

4 HUMAN BEHAVIOUR

Holiday hells

6 September 2006

One of the supposed joys of living in Cambridge is our proximity to Stansted and its limitless cheap flights to the stag and golf capitals of Europe. Quite how it has the brass neck to call itself "London Stansted" I don't know – I pity any poor foreigner jetting in and expecting a view of Big Ben as he taxis to his gate.

Of course, as well as tempting English hordes to Europe, Stansted also tempts European hordes to England – as is evidenced by the gangs of language students currently milling around the streets of Cambridge. They come to absorb our culture and language – and spend their fortnight snogging each other on Parker's Piece. It's probably French kissing as well. And they hire every bike Mike has to offer, and cycle en masse the wrong way up any street you care to mention.

On a recent trip of my own from Stansted, I took advantage of easyJet's new cabin baggage policy: as long as your bag comes within certain dimensions, it can weight whatever you like as long as can "lift it into the overhead locker without assistance". As my carefully-measured bag contained twelve tins of red salmon, 1.5kg of jumbo salted peanuts and the largest computer manual ever written (as requested by expatriate parent), I had to spend three weeks in the gym beforehand so that I could lift it effortlessly. My back will never recover.

On the same flight, I sat behind a couple with three young children: twin boys of about three and a girl of about five. (Mind you, I have no children and am only guessing – all I really know is that they were independently mobile, shrilly vocal and still happy to be seen with their parents, which means they could have been anything from two to eleven, really.) The two boys worked themselves into a lather of frenetic activity, chasing each other up and down the aisle, wrestling on the floor and tussling in that "s'mine, no, s'MINE!" manner over any toy. The parents, for some unfathomable reason, contributed to this by feeding them a steady stream of crisps, chocolate, sweeties and lemonade. Now I'm no scientist, but if you put lots of fizzy sugary liquid into a small container and then shake it violently, the result is explosive. And so it proved on descent, when twin #1 vomited copiously over dad, which caused twin #2 to share the experience with mum. And people ask why I don't have children.

Welcome to the Full-Price Forties

9 October 2006

As new anti-age discrimination legislation hits the headlines, I am reminded once again how galling it is to be middle-aged. The new law encourages people to think twice about calling colleagues "wet behind the ears" or "still in nappies" or "a bit long in the tooth" (although you'll be pleased to hear that you can still insult your nearest and dearest in the comfort of your own home – this is primarily workplace legislation). So now we have extra protection for the wet of ear and the long of tooth – but what about those of us stuck in the middle?

I call it the Full-Price Forties. Nearly every form of transport and attraction offers discounts to young people and students, and also to the old codgers (or super-experienced citizens, or whatever we're now supposed to call them). But when was the last time you turned up at a ticket office and the chap behind the counter said, "Hey, you look like a hard-working individual of middle years, paying your taxes and subsidising everyone else – can I offer you our Fabulous Forties Discount?" Ha – I thought not.

Actually, I'm not that bothered about it being a monetary discount – just a bit of special treatment would do. So cinemas could have dedicated Forties Film-Nights: movies likely to appeal to us (a good plot involving minimal technology, not too much graphic violence, just enough tasteful sex to give us a new idea or two, and some lovely scenery), to be watched with a nice glass of wine in hand – no rustling sweeties or popcorn, no mobile phones and no slurpy tonsil-cleansing in the back row. Similarly, clothes shops could put together ranges aimed at us: classic pieces in fine fabrics steering well clear of mutton-hood (no spaghetti straps, no witty slogans across the bust or bum, lots of clever hidden support and structuring) and nothing in size 8 except shoes.

So, marketing whiz-kids, I issue this challenge. We've had the Baby Boomers (poster child: Bill Clinton) and the MTV Generation (poster child: Pete Doherty, heaven help us). Task one: give us a good name – Full-Price Forties I fear is rather negative. And task two: make us feel loved and cherished. After all, you're relying on us for your inheritance.

You heard it here first

20 November 2006

I am a great listener-in to other people's conversations. I think I get it from my nan, who once made us stay on the bus four stops past her house because the couple sitting behind us were having such an absorbing discussion about what she coyly described to me as marital relations.

It's not that I chase people around town, earwigging on what they are saying, but Cambridge is such fertile ground for this hobby. There's the portly American tourist I passed on King's Parade who snapped about three hundred photos of King's Chapel and then said to his even more rotund wife, "It's sure pretty, but nothing compared to Little Rock Baptist Church". It wouldn't appear on my list of "sights to see before you die", but who knows. And there's the little girl who watched wide-eyed as a graduation crocodile went down Trinity Street and stage-whispered, "Mummy, look! It's the elves – but where's Father Christmas?"

Then I was walking past old Robert Sayle (the shop, not the man) and two very, very elderly ladies were waiting for a bus, bent almost double over their shopping trolleys. "Well, yes," said one to the other, shaking her head knowingly, "that's the problem with contraception". I've wondered about it ever since. And a few weeks ago I was bumbling around Sainsbury's in my usual fug of indecision when I squeezed past a new student making a call on his phone. "Mum," he hissed urgently. "What's in beans on toast?" Ah, the cream of our young intelligentsia (and cream contains cream, in case you're reading and wondering, young man).

Actually, mobile phones have been a godsend to nosy people like me. Only last week I heard a chap on the train explaining in very patient tones, "Bend your left leg – yes, the left. No, at the knee. How's that? Now the other one – careful you don't pull anything." Had his wife tied herself into a yoga knot, or got wedged into a small cupboard? Or perhaps it's the latest thing for very busy people: personal training by phone? That's one the frustrations of this hobby – you are often left wondering. All I need is to find the people who are listening in on the other sides of these conversations, and I'm in business – what a story that could make.

Thank you for reading this

21 January 2008

Regular readers will know that I am not averse to a little clothes shopping. Indeed, I can spend freely on the flimsiest of excuses – everyone needs a new pair of shoes to commemorate Presidents' Day (18 February), don't they? And surely you too treat yourself to a new handbag to mark the completion of the ironing? But now I have not an excuse, but an Iron-Clad Reason to buy a whole new outfit. For it appears that whatever I am currently wearing convinces people that I am, actually, a doorman.

Taught at a young age that it is impolite to let half a ton of steel and glass smack someone in the chops, I tend to hold doors open for those following me, expecting them to take the weight in their turn. But no – the majority sail through like the Queen Mary (ship, not monarch – although in some photos she does have a face like the back end of a battleship), leaving me standing there like a chump. This morning (hence the tirade) a family of four paraded through in line, and not one of them even acknowledged my presence. So I ask myself: is it unwise to wear a red frock coat with frogging and a black top hat when shopping in town?

I'm afraid the theme of politeness is not yet exhausted. At the weekend I went to my local recycling bins to drop off two bags full of paper. As I arrived, an old gent turned up with his bag. I offered to hold the bin lid open while he emptied his bag, and as he did, he tutted loudly. "The state of this area – it's a tip," he opined. I refrained from pointing out that yes, it was actually a tip – that's the point. "But then that's Cambridge these days," he continued. "Full of yobs. 64% of people living here are yobs. No manners, any of them." At which point he took his empty bag and left, leaving me holding the bin lid, two full bags at my feet, and no-one to hold the lid for me. And how does he know it's 64%? Is there a question on the census form that I have missed? "Are you now, or have you ever been, a yob? Or an ignorant old git? Or a doorman?" Harrumph.

Amorphous moaning

24 March 2008

In the evening, I'm something of a creature of habit. A monk's habit, actually, as my favourite item of clothing is my dressing gown, and I try to be in it by 6pm at the latest. It causes something of a stir on the train back from London, but it's not my fault that they don't provide changing facilities. A neighbour called round the other evening and commented, "Goodness – didn't you manage to get dressed today?". It occurred to me that perhaps I am sliding rather quickly towards those fur-lined bootees and that chair that lifts to tip you out when you need another cup of tea, and so I have decided to take greater advantage of the Cambridge night life.

Your idea of night life and mine might differ, so I'll clarify. I will not be darkening the door of anything that calls itself a "venue" or has an exclamation mark or misplaced colon in its name – such as Groove! or Re:mix. My main fear is that when I go in, the DJ (or whatever they call the nice chap who spins the platters) will spot me and announce, "Whoever has a mum who wears her dressing gown all day – she's here to collect you". No, rather I am planning to expose myself to the more cultural side of our town's offerings.

So last week I went along to a choral concert in a college chapel. I had heard of one of the composers on the programme (you can't go wrong with a German beginning with B) and thought it would be improving to hear something by the other chap, whose name I didn't know and now have no intention of remembering. We huddled in the chapel, wrapped in multiple layers to stave off the stone-chilled air (my dressing gown attracted plenty of envious glances, I can tell you) and in filed the choir and musicians. The conductor raised his baton, and on the first note we all levitated about two feet in the air.

Words like "atonal" and "discordant" don't begin to approach it. Ravens that had lived in the chapel belltower for centuries, thumbing their beaks at the dissolution of the monasteries, the Great Plague and even Margaret Thatcher, fled the building in terror. The audience sat through an endless twenty minutes of seemingly random notes, fingernails digging into the wooden pews. We spoke to one of the singers during the interval, and asked to see his music. Highlighted in green was his part: no specific notes, but rather a direction for "amorphous moaning". You and me both, matey.

The wrongs of rights

10 May 2010

Yesterday I walked up to the zebra crossing by the Jesus Green wooden bridge and dangled a tentative tootsie over the edge. A car approaching at about a thousand miles an hour screeched to a halt, and the driver leaned out of the window and yelled at me, "Oy! It's my right of way!". We then had a free and frank exchange of opinions, encompassing another driver, three more pedestrians and a dog who was desperate to get to the green and had his legs – and eventually his eyes – crossed.

What was sad about all of this was that the discussion about right of way had superseded all thoughts of courtesy and gallantry. The driver finally let me cross not because it was a nice, polite, generous thing to do, but because he was persuaded that it was indeed my right of way. (The dog's owner also murmured the words "solicitor" and "vehicular manslaughter", which may have helped my cause.)

Everyone is very quick to call up their rights as justification for almost any action but, as the courts are swiftly finding, nearly everyone's rights are incompatible with nearly everyone else's. The rock fan's rights to play thumping music in his own home are cancelled out by his neighbour's rights to get a good kip. A child's rights not to be excluded from the classroom are matched by his fellow pupils' rights to get an undisturbed education (and his teacher's rights not to be sent round the twist by the little toad). And that driver's rights to proceed across a striped portion of road without losing speed are trumped, I would suggest, by my rights not to be squished.

Rights are obviously important for important matters: I quite fancy not being imprisoned for no reason, or stripped of my citizenship. But for smaller matters, can't we go back to relying on kindness and common sense? So on the roads, how about instigating a pecking order similar to that in place on the high seas: the most vulnerable get priority. So lorries give way to buses give way to trucks give way to cars give way to motorbikes give way to bicycles give way to pedestrians. It certainly makes more sense than the current system, which seems to be exactly the same chain but in the reverse order. There's a name for that: bullying. And bullying can never be right.

The new queue

2 May 2011

Have you been to the new main post office in town? The one that has moved over the road? (Is Cambridge enrolled in some bizarre game of musical shops? What used to be the post office is now going to be Barclays, and what used to be Barclays is now Cath Kidston. Very confusing – unless you're the type of person who will go in for a mortgage and be happy to come out with a flower-patterned picnic rug instead.) Anyway, back to the post office. It seems at first glance to be lacking in one obvious feature: it has no external post box. The old post office had satisfyingly large mail slots outside – the sort that could take small children – but the new one has not even a normal pillar-box. So if you want to post something at our main post office out of hours, you have to break in to use the box inside. Say I sent you.

When you do go inside (legally, during working hours) you will find it a most unsettling experience. Rather than the reassuringly British queue, there is one of those take-a-numbered-ticket systems. And once you are clutching your ticket (and have noted dispiritedly that you are number 805 and the screen is showing number 4½), you just mill around. There is indeed a specific milling around area, with some squishy red chairs – most Continental. And every few minutes a mechanical voice says "Ticket 5 to window E", and everyone checks their ticket feverishly, like a bingo crowd on rollover night – even though you know you're ticket 805 (pay attention). At least with a queue you knew (literally) where you were, and you could while away the hours guessing whether the chap in front of you would buy one first class stamp (please oh please) or want to renew his passport and his road tax and change three thousand pounds in 2p pieces into Polish zloty (kill me now).

I once went on holiday to Havana, and in the bank there was a similar milling around system. But rather than the ticket machine, anyone who came in called out "¿Quién es último?" ("Who's last?"). Someone would stick up their hand, and you'd then know who was just before you in the queue, and when they got served (often days later – this was Cuba, after all), you were next. Go on, post office – let's go the whole cerdo*.

That's Spanish for hog

New wave cinema

14 November 2011

The flicks, the talkies, motion pictures, movies – call them what you like, I just love going to the cinema. And I know I'm biased, but I think we have one of the nicest cinemas around right here, with the Cambridge Arts Picturehouse. I've been a loyal customer from the days when they were in Market Passage, and all cinematic experiences were accompanied by the pungent aroma of French cooking from the restaurant upstairs and something much less appetising from the drains below. We didn't quite have an organist rising up through the stage to play along to the action, so I'm not that old thank you, but I have noticed a change in cinema etiquette over the years that I have been going.

I think people are confused, and it's not really their fault. What with home cinema systems and flat-screen tellies that cover a whole wall, cinemas have had to up their game to tempt the lardy of backside off their sofas. So now, rather than having to risk a whole ninety minutes without sustenance, you are permitted – nay, encouraged – to go into the showing with a coffee and a muffin, or a vat of fizziness and a silo of popcorn, or even a glass of wine or a pint and a packet of sea-salt and fresh cracked black pepper seasoned cashew nuts. (Get you – Maltesers not good enough for you any more?)

And if you make people this welcome, and encourage them to think that their comfort is paramount, you can't then be surprised if they treat the cinema like their own lounge. They chat to their friends. They loudly discuss where they've seen that actor before – you know, him off that thing on the telly. They text and even phone during the film. They get up and go to the loo – after all, that vat of fizziness has to go somewhere. And meanwhile some of us are Trying To Watch The Film.

Perhaps it all goes in cycles, like the width of men's ties. After all, in Elizabethan times people used to talk and drink and even gain carnal knowledge of each other during performances (which explains the voluminous petticoats). So perhaps when I next want to strangle my screen neighbour for clambering over me, I should instead imagine that I am part of an historical re-enactment and just be thankful that she's not peeing into her popcorn.

Would you marry him?

27 February 2012

A couple of weekends ago, I went to the cycling World Cup at the new Olympic velodrome in London; intended as an event to test the new facilities, it was also an opportunity for the cycling-mad to see our heroes in action. In the four seconds during which I was not staring at Chris Hoy's manly thighs, I happened to glance up at the big screen where they were relaying Twitter comments on the event, and someone had posted: "Debs will U marry me? x". What with Valentine's Day and the quadrennial appearance of the 29th February, this month is surely the top season for proposals of the marital variety.

In Cambridge, our local jewellery shops have gone into overdrive with their diamond ring window displays: I predict a worldwide shortage of red crêpe paper, frilly hearts and big-eyed teddy-bears. Restaurants have been offering special romantic menus, heavy on the champers, steak and oysters, and light on the garlic and spinach. Lads in long-term relationships must be feeling the pressure. But despite all this hinting and encouragement, I think that the element of surprise is important.

In an effort to nudge my then-boyfriend into proposing, I took us on a holiday in the summer of 1991 around the lovers' cities of Europe; I draped myself becomingly over fountains in Rome and moonlit bridges in Paris, I toyed playfully with ice-creams and fed him delicious morsels, I floated about the place in light summer dresses and dainty scarves, I even – Marilyn French forgive me – wore mascara. And when did he propose? During an ad break while we were watching a film on the telly, when I was wearing my pyjamas and boiling the kettle: "I'd better have decaf, otherwise I'll be up all night, and do you fancy getting married, then? And can you stop wearing that black stuff on your eyes?" I know: he's a silver-tongued devil.

With the benefit of more mature hindsight, I can see that what really matters is the essence of the proposal rather than its wrapping. And someone asking you to share the rest of their life is pretty amazingly romantic. As for Debs at the velodrome, we'll never know whether she did agree to marry her bike-barmy boyfriend. However, having been seduced by a cyclist myself, I do know that if she does agree she's in for a lifetime of bike bits in the lounge and Lycra dripping on the shower-rail. They don't tell you that at the jewellers.

Organised chaos

23 April 2012

The other morning, I found myself cycling through Cambridge at about 0858. As I tootled along Trinity Street, allowing myself to look at but not enter Heffers, I was like a lumbering whale in the middle of a dashing, sprinting, flashing school of speeding fish – other cyclists shot past me on both sides, at all angles, and dived into Green Street, Trinity Lane, Senate House Passage, Market Street or King's Parade, leaving me dizzy in their wake. And then I realised: this is the rush to lectures and shop-openings at 0900. I never saw it myself when I was a student because I react entirely differently to a deadline: I prepare so far in advance that I almost meet myself coming back, so by 0900 I was already waiting at my desk for everyone else to arrive. And then I went and married a man from the sprinting, final-minute school of deadline-assault, which can cause, to put it politely, friction.

Here's an example. Last week we both received our notices to submit a self-assessment tax return. (I know: you're filled with envy at our glamorous lifestyle – it is the stuff of which Posh and Becks merely dream.) I got out my diary, pinpointed a suitable day in June, and started a "tax return" folder for assembling all relevant documents. This is to meet the deadline of 31 January 2013. He, meanwhile, used his notice as a coaster for his coffee and then tossed it into the furthest reaches of his desk. My three desk-trays are labelled In, Out and Pending – his are Maybe, Fat Chance and Fuggedaboutit.

Sadly for those of us with a slavish devotion to deadlines, the discipline of planning is rarely seen as either laudable or exciting. Filofax does its best, with ad campaigns featuring stylish young things, but it's an uphill struggle. Rather, the impression is that brilliance is the by-product of a free-thinking mind, unfettered by such constraints as to-do lists and reminders. We say chaotic, you say untrammelled. Cambridge is stuffed with super-clever people who can imagine imaginary numbers and do instant translations from Greek into Latin and thence into Old Aramaic, but can't remember where they left their bikes or that milk goes off after, say, a fortnight on the windowsill. Everyone is full of praise for the double helix, but I bet it was Mrs Watson and Mrs Crick who had to put the bins out on the right day and return the library books on time.

Costume dramas

11 June 2012

Over the Jubilee weekend, I spent much of my time wearing a tiara – a four-inch high glittery extravaganza from Claire's. But it is surprising how quickly I got used to being in regal costume; in fact, I forgot I had it on at one stage and went to the Co-op in it – and no-one there made a comment (although perhaps that says more about our local Co-op than it does about my fancy headwear).

And then yesterday I took part in a classic car run from London to Brighton, driving my 1985 Renault 5 and dressed to match the era. Thanks to determined raids on local charity shops – and how infrequently do some people clear their wardrobes? – I wore a blue tiger-stripe stretchy mini-dress, an electric blue cropped jacket with power shoulder-pads and large gold buttons, black stilettos with Jackson Pollock paint splashes, and a chain-handled mock-leather shoulder bag containing a brick-sized mobile phone. Reader, I looked ridiculous. A mini-dress is particularly unforgiving of legs that belong on a cart-horse – thank heavens for American Tan tights.

What these two events have in common is that I looked daft – and I didn't care. As a teenager, I flatly refused to attend anything that required fancy dress, so afraid was I of looking silly. I missed parties at a Dutch friend's house, as they would have involved clogs and an orange wig. I never went trick or treating. I wasn't even that keen at university, and steered clear of toga parties, gathering of tarts and vicars (even the real ones) and Brideshead Bops (a craze at the time – you had to be there – or not, like me). But one of the compensations of growing older is that you just don't care so much about how you look.

For a start, you realise that the only one taking a real interest in how you look is you – and perhaps a husband, if you're lucky. No-one else really cares about how you look because they're all too busy worrying about how they look. And when I go back over photos of myself as a younger woman, I see that I was actually in pretty good shape: the lumps and bumps that I imagined blighted my appearance were literally imaginary. So if I looked better then than I thought I did, chances are that I look better now than I think I do – although perhaps I will just give that mini-dress back to the charity shop.

Little pleasures

10 September 2012

I should explain that my husband is away on business at the moment, otherwise he would be hearing this story – but as bankruptcy-inducing mobile roaming charges mean that we can speak to each other only in An Emergency, I will have to tell you instead.

Last night I cycled all the way home from the railway station (and I live near Mitcham's Corner) without stopping once. Every single traffic light was in my favour; no cars stopped in front of me to turn right; no pedestrians or cows made suicidal dashes/ambles across my path on Midsummer Common. And to make it even better, I had a fantastic tail-wind. From getting on my bike by the guided bus-stop (because I've realised that the only immobile objects available for bike-locking purposes after about 6.02am are the railings around the new trees in that part of the station) to sailing into my garage took me under eight minutes. It's my new PB, and probably a CR, OR and WR to boot. I'm still smiling.

It seems that the topic of happiness has been much debated in recent months, and what all the experts appear to agree on is that one of the best recommendations for a cheerful life is to take pleasure in small things. Anyone can be happy lying by a tropical pool or collecting their winnings from Camelot, but very little of our life is spent on holiday or having incredibly good luck. So rather than waiting for those brief moments, apparently we should enjoy the things that do happen every day.

Personally, I love bumbling around the garden in my dressing-gown first thing in the morning, checking for dead-heads and giving a decent burial to whatever little gift the cat has brought in overnight. My husband likes dissecting the bottom bracket of his bike and cleaning the ball bearings – very therapeutic, apparently, and it stops your bike and/or knees making that odd "klu-DUNK" sound with each turn of the pedals.

I also enjoy finishing things up, like finding that there's just enough spaghetti in the packet for our dinner, or emptying the dregs of one shampoo bottle into a new one. And last week, when Neil Armstrong's family said that we could all remember him by winking at the moon, I had such fun doing that every evening. Goodness knows what the neighbours thought – although they were probably just grateful that I was dressed.

Old friends are the best

21 January 2013

You know those glamorous, exciting people you see in documentaries and travelogues, the sort who carry everything they own in a small (airline regulation compatible) holdall and say things like, "I've never really settled anywhere – I'm a free spirit"? Well, that's not me. I am the exact opposite: wherever you plonk me, I immediately start trying to put down roots.

When we go on holiday, it takes me about four minutes to establish my favourite local restaurant, corner shop and view, and then I revisit them loyally every day. Like Frosties in the box, I like to settle. We moved into our current house "for a couple of years" in 1992 – and even though I call it our current house, just to make it sound as though I could move at any moment, you know and I know that it will take a shift in the underlying tectonic plate to get me out.

And just as I value familiar places, I treasure old friends. New friends are lovely too, but old ones – now they're something special. There are two main advantages to keeping hold of the people you have known for years. Firstly, you don't have to explain your background to them – and when you come from a family like mine, with so many marital reshuffles that it that makes Liz Taylor look like a one-man woman, that's a considerable time-saving. And secondly, they can remember how you used to be.

SUSAN IN THE CITY

My dearest friend and I met on our first day at secondary school, and whenever we are together we are eternally eleven years old. We giggle and snort at ridiculous things, we spend hours trying on clothes that we then don't buy, and we talk about love. We tell each other that we are gorgeous – like a young Audrey Hepburn (me) and Brigitte Bardot (her). But perhaps best of all, we still see in each other all the freshness and potential that we saw way back then. I encourage her to try out for the Olympic gymnastics team, and she reassures me that it's only a matter of time before Donny Osmond realises that I am the one for him.

As elderly relatives fall off the perch, it is friends who become the repository of our younger selves; soon this friend will be the only one who can remember what Susan at eleven was like, and by then I am sure to need reminding.

Getting the last word

22 August 2016

A friend's ten year old daughter, who wants to be an actress, dahling, recently asked me what was my dream job when I was ten. I took me a while to remember four decades back, but I seem to recall dithering between market researcher (I'd heard that it was good for people who liked maths) and professional high jumper (I had long thin legs and low body weight in those days – how the mighty have broadened). With the wisdom of age, I now know exactly what I would like to do: I'd love to be an obituarist.

I am addicted to obits. They are the first thing I read in any publication, be it the *Economist* for important people I have rarely heard of but who are (to my shame) enormously significant, or the *Guernsey Press* for locals I didn't know but who all died either "peacefully after a long illness bravely borne" or "suddenly". (What happens to the Guerns who die after a few weeks of feeling poorly and whinging about it, I don't know.) If I am stuck on a train with nothing to read, the online *Telegraph* obits are endlessly diverting, with their succinct headlines – "Kenneth Kramm, pharmacist who took the 'yuck' out of medicine" being a recent favourite. One Christmas my husband presented me with a thick obit collection called "Thinker, Failure, Soldier, Jailer" and I spent a wonderfully festive couple of days reading about lots of dead people.

SUSAN IN THE CITY

What appeals to me about the obit is its concision. The writer has to take someone's entire life and make a coherent story out of it, selecting the most telling details in order to indicate the particular uniqueness of that life. I adore doing research – even more than I like writing – so the idea of having to find out acres of information about someone in order to write only a few hundred words seems the perfect ratio to me.

Happiness experts (what? they exist) recommend writing your own obituary in order to determine the things in life you genuinely want to achieve, the things you'd really like people to remember about you. So here goes: Susan Grossey died, aged ninety, the day after being awarded an unprecedented fourth Man Booker prize. Her beloved husband was with her at the end, but died ten minutes after she did, saying he could not go on without her. (Sorry, love.)

5 HOME LIFE

I'm no bright spark

10 December 2007

Ask me about the energy efficiency of large electrical appliances. Go on, ask me: I could sit in that black leather chair and stare down old Jon Humphries on this one. For in the past month I have had much unwanted exposure to this side of the retail world. To be honest, I'm astonished to find that there is shopping I don't like, but there you have it.

First our washing-machine, after years of sterling service cleaning chamois-lined shorts and skin-tight jerseys (the kinkiness is all in your mind – we're cyclists, remember) gave up the watery ghost. We took ourselves to one of those big warehouse places on Newmarket Road – the sort of shop that Dante would have described as the previously-unimaginable tenth circle of hell, had they existed in fourteenth century

Florence. We carefully considered brand, colour, efficiency, price, noise, load and water consumption, before collapsing into a gibbering heap and pointing feebly at the nearest one. When it was delivered, the "point of delivery customer service satisfaction engineer" or whatever the drivers are called these days couldn't get out of the door fast enough. We understood why when we tried to unpack the machine and found that it had been dropped from a great height and was buckled beyond use. A mere twenty phone calls, one threat of legal action and two minor nervous breakdowns later, we had our replacement machine.

So imagine our delight when a week later the cooker conked out. Back to the tenth circle of hell? No fear! This time we took our much-battered credit card to a more upmarket establishment, imagining that our new cooker would arrive in an ermine-lined carriage drawn by four perfect white stallions, and be installed by George Clooney and his better-looking brother. (OK, when I say we, I probably mean I – my husband has the usual male aversion to getting in a "proper man" to do any work around the house, and reminded me that he has a Boy Scout badge in fire-starting and is therefore more than capable of plumbing in a cooker. Like you, I queried the term "plumbing in" but, unlike you, I have to live with the consequences of dissenting.) The reality could only be a disappointment, of course. So you must excuse me if I dash to get dinner organised – the queue in the chippy can be bad at this time of night. Well, you didn't think we were already plumbed in, did you?

'Twas the day before Christmas

24 December 2007

'Twas the day before Christmas, and all round the town
Every creature was stirring, rushing up street and down.
The shops were all threatening to shut tills at noon
And men started buying, not a moment too soon.

A bathrobe for mother, but better not dwell
On how like Les Dawson she'll look, or farewell
To the only idea that you've had for her gift
Unless you consider that deluxe stair-lift.

Dads are much simpler – a bottle will do,
Though he hasn't had gin since 2002
When he mixed it with lime and Joanna next door
Found him singing lewd hymns while face down on her
floor.

And as for the wife – it hardly bears thinking
What she'll have to unwrap, as your options are
shrinking.
Red knickers are cheap, vacuum cleaners are dull –
Please come, ideas, to your thick manly skull.

Whether it's hormones or brain cells, I'm really not
sure,
But most women finished shopping even before
The lights had been lit by a "Neighbours" starlet
(Which frankly's as low as our standards can get).

So now, dear reader, let the wrapping begin,
With sellotape stuck to your hands and your chin.

SUSAN IN THE CITY

How on earth do you cover a bike for the kids?
Or new saucepans for mum, complete with the lids?

And just when you've finished and poured a stiff drink
And flopped on the sofa, your mind starts to think….
O why didn't I label them up as I went?
Remembering what's what will take me 'til Lent.

The decos are up, so that's one less job,
And the spare room is ready for the ravening mob.
I'm sorry – I mean my delightful in-laws,
For whose multiple murder I'll soon have just cause.

The turkey is thawing on a tray in the shower,
With the cat planning raids, her aim to devour
As much as she can of the giblets and flesh
Before being sick and then starting a-fresh.

The same can be said of most of the crew,
Who will gorge on the biccies and grandpa's home
brew
While watching the film and waiting for lunch –
With parsnips and carrots and sprouts by the bunch.

And at last here's Her Maj with her words of good
cheer
As she wishes us joy and a happy new year.
I bet old Greek Phil's in the kitchen right now,
Basting that turkey with retsina, and how!

And so as we hurtle towards Christmas again,
Whether you love it, like me, or it drives you insane,
It gives me great pleasure to be able to write
Merry Christmas to all, and to all a good night!

What's in a name?

20 October 2008

I have written before of my disappointment with my first name – feeling it all the keener since discovering that I was named not after the beautiful Susan Hampshire, but rather after the Queen's favourite corgi, who went on honeymoon with Her Maj. My real beef is not with the canine nature of the name (it could be worse: one of the current pooches royal is called Bisto), but with its total unoriginality. I went on a knitting course recently, and five out of twelve of us were called Susan – in the end, we decided to call everyone Susan to save time. Frankly, I was having enough trouble with intarsia to bother remembering names as well. (No, intarsia is not an embarrassing itchy rash, but a fancy way of knitting with colour – although I'm betting that before long a WAG will be calling her offspring Intarsia Pacamac, or indeed Bisto.)

However, I am compensated by my surname. It is the source of endless amusement, as we see the latest mis-spelling on junk mail and hotel registers: I've had Glossy, Bossy, Crosby, Grassy, and – my personal favourite – Grottumbey. I once met a man called Robert Groffey and almost fell into his arms with delight: no matter how carefully I enunciate "gee ar o double-ess ee why" to people, they tend to hear "double-eff" in the middle – and here he was, my spelling twin. Oh, what a joy that double-barrelled name would have been.

SUSAN IN THE CITY

But the real benefit of such an unusual surname is that when you find someone else with it, you just know you're related. A chap contacted me last week via the *Cambridge News* website, saying "My mum was a Grossey, so I guess you're a cousin" – and I am. We've exchanged family trees, and it's a bit like being on my own version of "Who Do You Think You Are?" – except that no-one is paying for me to fly to the Caribbean to gaze pensively at gravestones and shed a mournful tear over the fate of people I hadn't heard of until four minutes ago.

Grosseys of old were farmers, brewers and radio telegraph operators – so far, so blah. But we've also found Peter Grossey the Pirate, lurking off the west coast of Africa three centuries ago and nicking gold from Spaniards – with "evil and mischievous intent", according to the judge who then promptly hanged him.

Taxing returns

22 June 2009

I'm a planner. Not for me the last-minute scamper towards a deadline; if I don't beat a deadline by at least a day, I consider that a rush job. It's a family trait: a cousin once got his jabs for an overseas trip so far in advance that he had to have them all done again at Heathrow because they'd expired before he set off. So getting a reminder that my tax return is due on 31 January 2010 was enough to send me scuttling to the filing cabinet last weekend to assemble the history of Grossey Financial 2008/09.

I've been self-employed for years now, so I know the routine. Remove cat from dining table (it's in the sun, so she languishes there like a Hollywood starlet on a chaise longue). Gather paperwork from banks, building societies, premium bonds, NatWest piggies, etc. and add up my interest for the past year. 17p. Remove cat from dining table again – she has shown her contempt for the revenue authorities by sitting on the return, flinging her leg over her head, and cleaning her nether portions. Look frantically for 28-digit security code for logging in to HMRConline – oooh, do you see the same pun as I do? Remove cat from keyboard before she admits to a salary of five billion pounds augmented with all-expenses-paid duck houses, swan lakes and emu mansions.

Work steadily through form, taking the view that if I don't understand the question, I probably didn't get the money. (Do I want to bring forward my unused losses from previous years? Eh? Are they taxing regrets these days?) Feel strangely guilty while signing the declaration, even though I know it's all true. And finally, wait impatiently for the system to work out how much I owe – nail-biting yet fascinating, a bit like those nature programmes where you know that one of the herd of big-eyed antelope sipping at the edge of the water is going to be scoffed by an alligator… but which one? Will I owe £3.48, or half the GDP of a small African state?

And then in the autumn, those ads with that nice Moira Stewart will come on the telly, reminding us to get our tax returns in on time, and I'll panic and think I've forgotten to do mine. You should see the pitying look the cat gives me as I go through it all again.

In your Facebook

7 September 2009

Regular readers will know that I am not the maternal type. When people ask whether I have children and I say no, they generally put their head on one side, lift their eyebrows in the middle and say pityingly, "Ah well, I'm sure there are plenty of other things you can do with your time." As I valiantly resist the urge to batter them to death with their own nappy-bags, I point out that – as I married into a large Catholic family – I have a wealth of nephews and nieces. (Our shorthand for them is "the niblings" – like siblings, but with a lot less teasing.) I've enjoyed being the auntie who supplies all the most inappropriate presents: one sister-in-law particularly welcomed the Dalek pyjama case that growled "Exterminate!" at random intervals throughout the night, propelling two young nephews into uncontrollable dawn hysteria. But now that the first wave of niblings are fully grown, I have discovered that the best way to keep up with them is to haul my middle-aged carcass into the digital era and join Facebook.

I know: the very concept smacks of the horror of seeing your dad trying to talk about (or worse, dance to) the latest music with your friends. When I signed up, tracked down the niblings and sent them friend requests, I fully expected them to thumb a virtual nose at me and direct me to the knitting and jam-making forum. But no: they have all graciously admitted me to their select group of friends (one niece has 956 friends

– is this possible? can she afford the Christmas cards?) and now I can track their antics and thoughts on a daily basis.

Actually, who am I kidding? It's more a minute-by-minute account of their every thought and experience. I'm quite interested to know that one nephew is moving house next week (at least, I think that's what "Off 2 me nu pad" means), but I'm less delighted with the information that another one experienced "red hot luuuuurve" last weekend. And the English teacher in me finds the whole txtspk a bit trying, although I am trying to lead by example. In response to the "nu pad" comment, I carefully posted on my nephew's wall: "Delighted to hear that you are moving house: I wish you every happiness in your new abode". Ten minutes later, someone else had added: "Hooz the old lady – yr gran?". Blstd chk!

Peel for your life

11 January 2010

Once upon a time, there was a young girl. Her parents had separated, and so she was the only child of a single mother. Christmasses, although festive, were fairly quiet – one granny, one uncle, one mother, one spoilt little girl. (Honesty is its own reward, apparently.) Our heroine grew up and fell in love, but she forgot to ask the one question every girl should ask her swain. No, not "Do these car seats recline?", but "Do you come from a large and fecund family, devoted equally to going forth and multiplying and to gathering the clans together each and every Christmas for a shindig that will stretch both the waistband and the nerves to breaking point?". Had I asked this (for, dear reader, that little girl was I), perhaps I would have risen from that reclining seat and run for the hills.

At the massing of the, well, masses this year, there were thirty-two of us. Twelve were aged ten and under, and most of the others acted ten or under. The noise levels were astronomical. The youngest attendees learnt quickly to hang around the door and greet each new arrival with "Merrychristmaswheresmypresent?" – piranhas could not have stripped flesh from a minor Bond character more efficiently.

Usually I sit in the middle of this swirling mass of in-laws, wondering whether this is the year I should take up drinking, and tapping my watch significantly every time my husband heaves into view. But this year I cracked it, thanks to a tip from a similarly overwhelmed friend. "Peel things," she recommended. "Volunteer to peel things."

So Christmas 2009 saw me standing in the corner of the kitchen, back to the chaos, soothing Radio 4 murmuring away beside me, peeling enough potatoes and parsnips and carrots and beetroot and, for all I know, small children to feed the ever-gaping maw of the family Christmas. And when the peelables ran out, I started chopping, then I moved on to dicing salad for Boxing Day. I had hands like prunes, but I preserved my sanity. And my mother-in-law surveyed the several hundred-weight of veggies that had passed through my grip, and said (I'll quote this in full, so you can all witness it) "What a marvellous daughter-in-law you are!" (Considering she still talks wistfully of the girlfriend my husband had in 1987, this is real progress.) And then she ruined it all by adding, "You can come again next year!" Aaaaaargh!

Pas de pub*

8 March 2010

I am stuck in the seventh circle of recycling hell. The usual half-kilo of flyers, leaflets, menus, invitations and adverts thumped through my letter-box yesterday evening. As I was putting the load straight into the bag where we collect paper for recycling, I noticed that several of the afore-mentioned flyers, etc. proudly proclaimed "Printed on recycled paper". It's probably the very same paper that I hauled to the recycling bin last week.

I don't know how to put this nicely: I hate junk mail. Frankly, for me, the clue is in the name. I have never bought anything from anyone calling at the door – not even those "bargain" tea-towels and dusters, or double-glazing from the chap who offered to replace my lovely antique sash windows with "strong plastic windows that will look almost the same but a bit more modern, and without the sash effect" – and I'm even less likely to respond to an ad pushed through the door.

Those multi-coloured menus are the worst of all, especially when they offer you mind-boggling amounts of food in a form of a "family feast" (this presumably explains the hereditary nature of heart disease) or (regular readers will know my hatred of this) delivered in a bucket. Food should see the inside of a bucket rarely on the way out – and then only in extremis or at university – and never on the way in. And it's all so random: on the same day I received leaflets advertising a bowling alley and a mobility scooter. If I could use one, I wouldn't need the other. I particularly loathe junk mail that requires me to do something. If you deliver to me an unasked-for catalogue or bin bag, that's your lookout: don't instruct me to leave it on the doorstep on a day of your choosing.

I'm going to ask the council to rig up an underground chute that goes direct from my letter-box, sifting out anything that is not in an addressed envelope, and conveying it straight to the space-age recycling bins on Chesterton Road. Failing that, I might do what a Dutch friend of mine has done for years with great relish: he collects his junk mail, sorts it by source, and once a year posts it back to the relevant restaurant or hairdresser or mobility scooter seller, without a stamp on the envelope, and enclosing a leaflet advertising his own gardening business.

* That's what the canny French write on their letterboxes –
it means "no junk mail"

My own little banking crisis

23 August 2010

I'm one of those odd people who panic disproportionately about small things but weather large disasters with sang froid. So if I forget to buy milk I chastise myself for hours, but I can meet the recent economic meltdown with calm and equanimity. When the news comes on, with that peculiar Peston chap and his scary graphs and downward plunging arrows, I take the view that there's little I can do about it, and my buying or not buying a punnet of strawberries is not going to affect our economy in the slightest.

What I have learnt, however, is that banks are not infallible. You may wonder how I reached my great age without realising this sooner, but the first film I ever saw was "Mary Poppins", and the father – Mr Banks – was a bank manager and they lived in a lovely house and could afford Julie Andrews to look after their kids. And my favourite books were about Paddington Bear, who lived with the Browns, and Mr Brown was a bank manager. So the die was set early for me: comforting home environment = bank manager = good. (I'm also well-disposed to chimney sweeps and marmalade, for the same reason.) So it was certainly a shock to find that money given trustingly into the gentle care of the Messrs Banks and Brown of today could just disappear.

I decided to take financial action. I read up about protection limits and premium bonds, about ISAs and Iceland. I listened to the wise words of financial gurus and my London cabbie. Finally I grasped that – rather than foolishly staying loyal to one bank and expecting them to repay the favour – the key is to spread your risk, and so I opened several other bank accounts and shared my money between them. My husband chose different banks, so that if my banks collapse, he can support me. (I think he imagines it will work the other way round, but show me the contract, sucker!) I sat back and looked smugly at the wide array of institutions now holding my money, each account nestling carefully under the protection threshold. OK, so it takes me hours longer each month to go through all the statements and paperwork, but I've spread my risk as instructed.

And then giant Spanish bank Santander swooped in and bought every single one of my banks. Back to cuadro uno, as they say in Madrid.

Meltdown

4 July 2011

By the time you read this it will doubtless be a distant memory, but I am writing in the grip of a heat-wave. Thankfully we live in a very elderly house, so our thick walls keep us cool and the total lack of match between doors and frames allows the air to circulate, but it has been amusing to see how Cambridge reacts to what the weatherman enjoys calling soaring temperatures. It's sardine city out there on Jesus Green, with people stripping down to the essentials (and in many cases unwisely beyond them) and slathering themselves in factor 20. The river is crammed with punts, canoes, barges and rafts, as the sweaty do what they can to get close to the water. And apparently it is standing room only in Jesus Green pool – which is a shame, as it's very deep.

In the town centre, the usual signs of a meltdown are in place. The supermarket shelves have been denuded of ice-cream, salad, strawberries and those portable barbecues which deliver the unusual taste sensation of scorched/bloody. There isn't a pair of flip-flops or board shorts to be had for love nor money. And the shops have their window displays of back-to-school stationery items and winter woollies. It turns out – who could have foreseen it, with all that glass – that the Grand Arcade is in fact a giant greenhouse, with the attendant oppressive atmosphere. And the most efficient air-conditioning in town belongs to John Lewis, who have cleverly scheduled their clearance (toff-speak for sale) to take full advantage of the weakened condition of those driven to seek refuge from the torrid temperatures. Meanwhile, those trying to escape to the capital were foiled by overhead cables on the railways, which sagged in the sizzling conditions.

In short, we melted, collapsed and gave up the ghost. And all because the thermometer climbed to 30 degrees. Phew. That's the sort of temperature that prompts Egyptians to slip on a little cardi, while Bahrainis would huddle together for warmth. Whatever happened to the stoic Brit, taking whatever nature throws at him with a stiffening of the lip and a bracing cup of tea? We enjoy one of the most equable climates in the world – as Goldilocks would have it, not too hot, not too cold – and yet we can't seem to cope. Heaven help us if we ever get a tsunami or an ice-storm.

Power from the people

29 August 2011

Yesterday I was working hard at my desk – well, those YouTube videos of sneezing pandas don't watch themselves, you know – when the screen flickered and died. I looked disbelievingly at my hands in case I had had some sort of chocolate-induced spasm and hit a weird combination of keys, but then noticed that my gently-humming printer had gone quiet. Power cut! Now where did I put those candles – and why would I need them at ten in the morning?

I looked out into the street and it was like a row of cuckoo clocks: heads were appearing from every door. A chorus of "Are you off too?" quickly established that we were all electricity-free. Power cuts were quite common when I was little, hence my instinctive search for candles – although I'm not sure that the lightly-scented bergamot and tangerine "bougie de relaxation" that I finally unearthed in the cupboard quite cuts the mustard in the illumination stakes. But these days outages are quite rare, and usually heralded by a flurry of warnings from the electricity company, so this unexpected withdrawal of power was a bit worrying.

And then I started thinking. My computer was off, so that pretty much knocked my work/pandas on the head. I couldn't do the ironing or the hoovering, or even put on a load of washing. Without the telly, I couldn't catch up on all those improving documentaries I keep recording about science and maths and the environment (and then eschewing in favour of DVDs of "Dallas" and anything by Richard Curtis). And with the freezer now off, I really ought to eat that ice-cream. So it made sense, nay, it was my housewifely duty to sit in the garden with a magazine and eat a big bowl of Ben and Jerry's. And then the dratted power came back on again.

Of course this meant going around the house and resetting all the clocks. It seems that every single electrical device, probably including the toaster, has a clock that gaily reverts to a flashing 00:00 whenever there is a sniff of a power cut. All the phones were blinking at me, which made me wonder: if you do lose power and all your communication devices are electrical (phone, email, fax), how do you let anyone know? I wonder whether bergamot and tangerine candles can send smoke signals – fragrant ones, of course.

Susan on the Shelves

22 July 2013

I like to think that, over the years, you and I have become friends. I've admitted to my many and various foibles (Jaffa Cakes, shoes, rose-scented toiletries, magazines – all at the same time if possible, please) and you have smiled indulgently and thanked your lucky stars that I am just a distant columnist and not a close relative. But now I have to confess that I have been keeping a secret from you. For the past four years I have been writing a book.

Whenever possible, I was sneaking off to my own little piece of heaven: a desk on the fifth floor of the University Library, overlooking King's, with a sturdy radiator for winter and an opening window for summer. You may remember that I used to hanker after the café lifestyle, sitting in the corner of a coffee emporium, sipping on a frothamochaccino while jotting bon mots in my Moleskine notebook. But it turns out that this fantasy has many drawbacks. I don't like coffee, for a start, and the constant noise and movement in such watering-holes is just too distracting. And my writing is so atrocious that anything scribbled in a Moleskine is lost to posterity through illegibility. So in order to get anything done I need to sit in silence at a laptop – hence the fifth floor hideaway.

So why haven't I blabbed about my book before? Normally, as my husband sometimes comments when he reads yet another marital secret laid bare in the *Cambridge News*, it's no sooner the word than the column. The truth is, I didn't want to tell anyone in case I didn't finish it – in case I threw the whole lot from the library ramparts and went for a cheese scone in the tearoom. But I did finish it, buoyed up by multiple Star Bars, and one of the utter joys of living in a bookish city is that other people are genuinely pleased for me.

I'm still reeling from the excitement of seeing my book in a real shop, but I can now report that both G David's and Heffers are stocking "Fatal Forgery", and both booksellers seem almost as happy about the self-published local author concept as I am. There is, however, one downside: writing and publishing a book turns out to be such terrific fun that now I want to do it all over again.

Knever again

30 June 2014

Knitting used to be a thrifty hobby; homemade jumpers were a cheaper alternative to their factory-made and shop-bought brethren. But no longer: as the price of shop woollens has gone down, that of balls of yarn and patterns has risen, and it is now the luxury alternative to make your own.

Despite this, I love knitting: I find it restful, it allows me to justify trashy telly if it is accompanied by an evening of productive knitting, and it is a creative outlet for those of us with the artistic skills of a rice pudding. Thus far I have limited myself to knitting tops for myself and female friends, and (when the trashy telly needs a bit more concentration) scarves. A few weeks ago, however, when I suggested my husband should think about presents for his forthcoming significant birthday, he asked for a hand-knitted jumper.

The palaver, ladies and gentleman! Thankfully the range of patterns for men's jumpers is not nearly as extensive as that for women, otherwise we'd still be choosing. We went through every book of men's designs, looking at photos of chaps in manly poses (leaning on barn doors, sitting astride vintage motorbikes, gazing into the distance over choppy seas) while my husband tried to decide which would make him look most rugged or moody or brooding. He eventually selected a partly cabled affair – big chunky cables, as apparently smaller ones look girly. Then for over an hour we stood in the woolly bit of John Lewis [other department stores are available – but not in Cambridge] while he examined the yarn selection, squeezing each ball [of yarn] and then holding it against his cheek, eyes closed, to check it for softness. Yarn chosen, we moved on to colour.

His brief? "Something bright, but not too bright, and a bit flecky and natural-ish." I found myself standing behind him while he looked into a mirror, and bringing two handfuls of each colour of yarn round in front so that he could envisage it knitted up into "his" jumper and see if it "went with his eyes". Finally, a decision was made – denim-ish blue, in case you're curious – and I bought the enormous number of balls required to encase the male torso.

Every evening since then, he has looked along the sofa balefully as I finish my current knitting project, and said in a small voice, "When will you start *my* jumper?" Give me knitting strength.

Mountains out of molehills

18 May 2015

I have recently learnt something about myself. If faced with an actual crisis, I am actually rather a good person to have around: calm, clear-thinking and (let's be honest) bossy. So if someone has an accident in my vicinity, I quickly take both stock and charge and then issue instructions like billy-o. But if the crisis is only potential rather than real, my reaction is to worry at it like a dog with a bone and blow it up into something much more ghastly than the reality could ever be. In short, I am a catastrophist.

As exhibit one I present our bathroom. I was soaking in the bath the other day when I felt a little roughness on its surface. A small patch of enamel – about the size of a 5p coin – had chipped off. This is an elderly metal bath that has already been resurfaced at least three times so its days of a flawless complexion are numbered (I can sympathise). But it's a built-in bath, so replacing it would necessitate ripping out lots of surrounding tiles… which are connected to the wall tiles, which join up with almost every surface of the bathroom. In other words, we would need to gut the bathroom – our only bathroom and loo. So it's co-ordinated loo visits to local hostelries and several weeks of sponge baths, or moving out.

The bathroom and kitchen are located in our single-storey extension, and since we moved in almost every other house in the street has upgraded to a two-storey extension. So if we're doing big works on the bathroom which would require us to move out anyway, we might as well add the extra floor – planning permission permitting. And if the extension is going to be that tall, why don't we fill in the small bit of garden that would be enclosed in the "elbow" of the extension to extend the lounge and maybe add an upstairs loo for when we're doddery?

By now I realised that the water was rather cold, and in the space of ten minutes I had gone from a small chip in the enamel to three extra rooms, a spirited tussle with the planning committee, and imminent retirement. I took a deep breath, and reasoned that as long as the bath is still watertight it is probably fulfilling its main function, so I threw out the extension with the bathwater.

The Birdman of Cambridge

28 September 2015

Don't let anyone tell you that life in a Cambridge terraced street is uneventful. I was sitting knitting (see – drama already) when I heard a scrabbling noise as something lost its grip in our chimney and landed in our cast-iron stove in the fireplace. Now, this hasn't been used for about two years so for all I know there was a family of Hobbits living in there. I approached with trepidation, opened the doors at the front and shone in a handy bike-light – but nothing. I then recalled my hour-long lesson on "how to light the stove" delivered optimistically by my husband some years ago, and opened the baffle – the plate that allows or blocks air from the chimney – and into view came a bird. I looked at him (her?) and s/he looked at me. Neither of us was particularly taken. I closed the doors and considered.

If I just reached in and grabbed the bird – even if my arm could work at that angle – s/he might (a) peck me a lot, (b) fly back up the chimney, (c) take fright and burst out into the lounge, shedding feathers, soot and poo en route, or (d) die of fright. None of these was an attractive outcome. So I locked the cat in the bedroom, draped a calming towel over the open stove doors, scattered some bird peanuts inside (I'm nothing if not a good hostess – always offer your guests refreshment) and went to fetch the neighbour.

I am lucky enough to live next door to people who are keen ornithologists, and I thought they might know how to avoid options (a) to (d) and instead effect a satisfactory rescue. The birdman answered the door. "What type of bird is it?" he asked, not unreasonably. "Wings – beak," I offered.

He took one look inside my stove and declared it a lady blackbird. By then, my blackbird guest had hopped forward a little to inspect those peanuts. My neighbour reached in fearlessly, and the bird flew past us both and head-butted the window. I feared the worst, but it simply stunned her enough to allow the neighbour to grab her and take her into the garden, murmuring sweet blackbird nothings. He opened his hands, and she flew off without hesitation, and went straight over the garden wall to the sumptuous bird smorgasbord on offer in his garden. So that was it: she simply had the wrong address.

Share and share alike the Dutch

7 December 2015

I've just bought my husband's Christmas present.
It's a drill. And no, that hasn't spoilt the surprise
because he led me to it in the shop, pointed out all of
its marvellous features – apparently these things create
holes in walls – and then coyly looked away at the till as
I paid for it. The torture for him is that he can see it
sitting under my desk, but he's not allowed to touch it,
read the instructions (as if he would!) or drill any holes
in any walls until after breakfast on Christmas Day. My
drill, my rules. But as we were wandering the endless
aisles of orange and black power-tools, I mused that we
could learn a lesson from the Dutch.

I have a friend who is married to a Dutchman of
the traditional variety: they live in the village where he,
his parents and his grandparents were born; their house
is a riot of orange every Konigsdag; he plays billiards at
the local bar; and they share all manner of things with
their neighbours. For instance, when a Dutch baby is
born, it is traditional to stand a six-foot wooden pink or
blue stork in the front garden, with the name of the
new arrival chalked on its beak. Buying such an item
for use once or twice would be madness, so every
Dutch neighbourhood has a pair of these that you can
borrow, stored in the local community centre.
Similarly, when you turn fifty and become an
"Abraham", there is a large wooden bearded man that
your friends will amusingly prop up outside your house

– strangely, I found this custom much more endearing before I myself reached my late-mid-forties.

And also shared are occasional use items like lawnmowers, strimmers, leaf-blowers, power-washers, drills and so on. What a clever scheme. Not only does it appeal to the frugal nature of the Dutch – why tie up capital in items that you use so rarely? – but also it clears space in their garages and sheds for more useful items, like billiards tables and fridges full of beer and large collections of wonderful bicycles.

I'm sure we can all contribute things to our own community that we use infrequently. For my part, I'm happy to turn in my food mixer, one of our three(!) sandwich toasters, a juicer and a fondue set. Please don't judge me.

The big lifestyle con

22 February 2016

One of my favourite places in Cambridge for a wander is the top two floors of John Lewis. I often park my husband in the café while I go off to immerse myself in the promise of a lifestyle. Over these two floors, disguised as cushions and snuggly throws and stylish sofas, are my dreams of how life could – perhaps should – look.

It's the same dream they're peddling in the décor pages of women's magazines, and the furniture and bathroom ads on telly. You remember it: you step into your warm and tidy home, your toes sinking into the deliciously soft yet artfully handmade rug. Your spacious kitchen/diner is bathed in light, and you turn on the gleaming coffee machine while bumping that soft-slide drawer closed with your hip, smiling beatifically (some might say smugly) all the while. You then settle onto the nicely plumped-up sofa, whose cushions are in just the right place, and raise the steaming mug to your lips while your well-behaved pedigree cat curls in your lap. You both purr contentedly.

Now let me tell you what really happens in our house. I get home and remember, from the icy chill that greets me, that I once again forgot to put the heating on timer. One of the joys of living in an old house is that nothing quite fits, and the winter wind whistles round the front door. I turn on the light in our decidedly un-spacious kitchen, and the bulb blows. As

SUSAN IN THE CITY

I am scrabbling around in the under-stair cupboard for a spare, our un-pedigree moggy barrels in through the cat-flap, dancing muddy paws across the floor, to tell me that (a) she is hungry and wants dinner NOW otherwise I can forget about purring for quite some time, and (b) she has been sick on the landing. You don't see that on the top floor of Johnny Lou-Lou.

And yet, decades of reality does not stop me yearning for this glamorous alternative. Every few years I convince myself that all I need to achieve lifestyle perfection is a really thick heritage-style eiderdown and a mountain of cushions – for Sunday morning lie-ins with the papers – and they last about three weeks until my husband roars that he is suffocating in his own bed and banishes them to the loft. Perhaps that's my answer: the lifestyle of my dreams in actually in my loft.

Tricky treating

28 November 2016

It sometimes seems that the year is one long progression of confectionary-based festivals: no sooner have the shops cleared the Christmas selection boxes from the shelves than they are stacking them with heart-shaped goodies, which in turn give way almost seamlessly to Easter eggs. To be fair, I remember all three of these from childhood – although the gap between them was actually discernible with the naked eye. But the one that baffles me, as an Englishwoman of fifty, is Hallowe'en. In my teens I was friends with two American sisters who went trick or treating, but my parents were of the view that it is confusing to children to warn them about taking sweets from strangers for 364 days of the year and then encourage them to do it on one particular night, and refused to let me join in the ritual demanding of candy with menaces.

In recent years, however, Hallowe'en has really taken off in England. From a child's perspective, of course, what's not to like? You get to dress up and gorge on sweets. But what does it really mean? It seems to be a blend of some unfamiliar religion – worshipping the dead and calling up the undead – with a rather limited harvest festival concentrating exclusively on the pumpkin. And let's face it, England in late October is not the ideal location for gangs of children to be roaming the streets – it's dark, almost certainly wet, and people would rather stay cosy in the lounge than answer the doorbell to yet another gaggle of mini witches and Harry Potters. Bonfire Night is much more our thing: you wrap up warm, wave a sparkler around a bit dangerously, and eat an undercooked burger on the way home.

And perhaps other people are coming around to my curmudgeonly way of thinking. This year I sighed deeply in the supermarket and caved in to the pressure of the displays to lay in stocks for our costumed visitors, splashing out a whole four pounds on various colourful bags of pure sugar. At home I decanted them into our mixing bowl and slapped away my husband's hand whenever it crept near. On the evening in question we turned on our hall light to indicate that we were At Home to callers. Reader, not a single boy wizard knocked on our door, and we're still working our way through that bowl of dental horrors.

6 CAMBRIDGE

The Cambridge year

18 September 2006

It is inevitable that a city as venerable and unique as Cambridge will have its own rhythm. The Cambridge year starts in October; the streets fill with eager, bright-eyed new students, having deep conversations over half a shandy and wobbling around on their bikes. November hits them hard, when they realise how cold it can be out here in the Fens, and Sainsbury's experiences its annual run on hot chocolate and crumpets. In December, you can't get a seat in a local restaurant, as everywhere is packed with office groups chucking down (and later, up) the house plonk and groping each other unwisely under the table.

January is for gentle reflection, as we try to remember why we chose to live in a place buffeted by winds blowing straight from the Urals. The streets run red in February, as the commercial guilt-fest that is Valentine's Day takes hold and the MDs of Thornton's and Hallmark put down-payments on their new yachts. March sees the Cam being worked into a froth by hardy souls in freezing boats practising to bash each other out of the way and gain the Head of the River (whatever that may be).

Things go quiet in April, when those eager students realise that all the aforementioned revelling has left them sadly lacking in the knowledge department, and exams are next month. May catches the tourists out, as they descend in camera-clicking crowds expecting warm weather (tee hee) and May Balls (double tee hee). In June, the May Balls, entertainments, extravaganzas, romps and orgies take place, and shortly after that the town becomes clogged with Volvos and Range Rovers packed to the gunwales with student paraphernalia, as Jonquil and Cassandra return whence they came for a summer of jolly japes.

In July, fleets of coaches disgorge along the Backs, the tourists imbibing the learned atmosphere for about ten minutes before heading to Starbucks, McDonalds and Gap. August sees a slight change in emphasis, when language students arrive en masse (note my facility with other languages) and spend 68p between them during a two-week visit to learn English, apparently by wearing jaunty matching rucksacks and having sex with each other. And then comes September, my favourite Cambridge month. The punt pimps pack up and Cambridge becomes an ordinary working city – that is, if you think it's ordinary to go to work in a black gown, or a red gown and top hat, or morning dress.

Park life

25 February 2008

I was in Paris a few weekends ago, and – beautiful city though it certainly is – it compares very poorly with Cambridge in one important regard. Paris has several urban parks, but they are not parks in the useful sense. They lack a certain je ne sais quoi – perhaps, oh, grass. Parisian jardins are dusty, pebbly affairs, with occasional tiny patches of green fenced off from human contact (although that doesn't stop the elegant ladies from dropping their handbag hounds onto this preserved grass for "le poop").

Cambridge, on the other hand, is bursting with what councils like to term "green spaces", each with its own character. My local one is Jesus Green, which starts to give value right at the outset: there's little that's more fun than directing a tourist to "turn right at Jesus" – just watch them nod nervously as they back away. The tennis courts are an excellent showcase for the full range of gentleman's shorts, from the Indian Army baggies to the eye-watering Bjorn Borg snugs. The sign that has appeared asking people not to feed bread to the wildfowl gives rise to all sorts of subterfuge: dad drapes himself casually across the sign while mum and kids guiltily hurl Warburtons at the ducks, and I swear the swans are planning an editing attack on the sign itself, hoping to scratch out the word "not" with their beaks. Various hurling games are much in evidence, from the laid-back Frisbee crew to the rampaging lacrosse players who – for reasons best known to themselves – play across the main path, which adds a certain frisson to any traverse of the green, as you wonder whether the last thing you'll hear in this world before being decapitated by the speeding ball is "Oh, good crosse, Jacinta!".

I am also fond of other Cambridge parks. Midsummer Common is the slightly edgier, rougher big brother to Jesus Green. I've always been tempted to buy a few sheep and graze them there, as is my right as a city resident, and was delighted when a local vet did in fact introduce a small herd of red cows. Townie that I am, it took me a while to realise why their numbers were dwindling…

Parker's Piece is probably the most mathematically pleasing of our green spaces, being almost square with paths around all four edges and from corner to corner. And although the Parisians make a big fuss about the Eiffel Tower, frankly, I think the dolphins are better on Reality Checkpoint.

Lights, camera, Cambridge!

8 December 2008

Cambridge is old and picturesque so it is no surprise that our lovely town regularly appears on both the silver and small screens. A few dreamy shots of punters going past King's is useful movie-maker shorthand for either (a) the ultimate in Englishness, or (b) clever people solving very tricky theorems, or even (c) weak-willed young toffs who aren't really all that interested in women but think that Moscow is a nice place for a holiday.

But what you see on screen is very rarely the real Cambridge. When I was a student here, we stumbled across Maureen Lipman filming "Eskimo Day", about parents bringing children to Cambridge for interviews. When we breathlessly gathered around the college telly some months later (ah yes, those under-privileged days before everyone had their own telly), we watched Maureen turning the corner from All Saint's Passage and ending up in front of King's.

More recently I took maidenly delight in seeing David Tennant strolling around town in an earnest manner and Edwardian knee-breeches. "Einstein and Eddington" was finally broadcast last week – and what is this Cambridge of which we speak? Our David rockets around town on his sturdy bicycle, scattering honest townspeople in his wake, and obviously using some of his Time Lord powers to rearrange space to suit him. He pedals furiously up and down All Saint's Passage, dashes into the front of Corpus, comes out the back of John's, strolls thoughtfully over the Bridge of Sighs, and lives in some enormous grey-stoned mansion that claims to be the observatory. Most damning of all, he is shown cycling up a hill – a HILL, I tell you. Next you'll be telling me that the real Einstein did not bear an uncanny resemblance to Charlie Chaplin.

But perhaps the most egregious misrepresentation ever of Cambridge on celluloid is in "Chariots of Fire" (admit it – you're already humming the slo-mo beach music, aren't you?). Picture the scene: plucky Harold Abrahams overcomes class and religious prejudice to get to university, and agrees to take the challenge of running around the perimeter of Trinity Great Court within the tolls of the noon bell. The first bell tolls, he runs, his legs going like the clappers, the bell clappers going like, well, the clappers – and he does it! But wait – it appears that he has in fact run around Eton College in Berkshire. Perhaps he was reading geography.

Just after this column was printed, I received a lovely letter (my second) from reader Patrick Mills of Cambridge, in which he shared a bit of local history: "A long time ago I had the job of winding the clock in Great St Mary's when the official winder (known as the 'steeple keeper') was too busy (he was also a sub-postmaster). It certainly was a big physical effort. On another occasion I was recruited to pump the 'University' organ in the same church. Needless to say, both organ and clock have long since been electrified."

Happy birthday to U

25 January 2010

I'm not what you would call a night-owl. If we're honest, I'm not even much of an evening budgie. If I'm not in my dressing gown and fluffy mules/duvet boots (delete according to season) by the time Susie Fowler-Watt is saying hello on the 6.30 edition of "Look East", I think I'm straying into Michael Howard territory, with something of the night about me. So it took something really special to get me to turf out of my cosy bolt-hole on a chilly January night – but then, the university in your home town doesn't turn 800 years old every day of the year.

Well, actually, it does, because the Varsity Big Birthday Bash Planning Committee (probably not their official title, but you get the drift) did what I long to do for my own birthday: they stretched the celebrations out over a whole year. And the end of it all on was marked on 17th January with a fabulous light and fire show. (Personally, I would have been a bit nervous with all those flaming torches being tossed around near King's College Chapel and the wooden-framed buildings of King's Parade, but hey ho.)

Like hundreds of others, we queued up to walk the route past the Senate House and round the back of King's. Unlike hundreds of others, I found myself being asked several times, "How long will the route take?" and "When's the next fire show?" Then I realised that my new bright orange mac – bought specifically to keep me safe on the old penny farthing –

was remarkably similar to the dayglo jackets worn by the crowd control chaps. I love the idea of a group of academics and various well-behaved townsfolk needing crowd control – there's nothing like a crazed horde of people muffled in coats, traipsing slowly past your building, gazing at the stained glass and going "Oooooh – pretty!".

And very handy those academics were too. While I was puzzling over one particular pattern being projected onto the back of King's, someone behind me said sagely, "Ah yes – the upper brain stem in cross-section" – so that's nice, just before dinner. And a laser playing on the surface of the river was kindly interpreted by another clever-clogs as the orbit of the earth around the sun – and here's me thinking it was spelling out "Sponsored by Barclays". It's good to know that the 800 years of book learning has not gone to waste – or at least, not for some.

Losing track of time

1 February 2010

The other day I walked from Mitcham's Corner to John Lewis. (There is a columnist in a London newspaper who frequently mentions that her favourite shop is Johnny Lou-Lou, and it took me months to realise where she meant. Mind you, in my family, we buy our food from Snozzo's and our stationery from Wiffsmiths.) Anyway, it was a perishing day and I was wearing the sort of thick gloves that make it impossible to do anything once they are on – even take them off again. I needed to know the time, but of course could not excavate my watch from the depths of the gloves. I know, I thought: I will look out for a clock. And you will be as amazed as I was to learn that I walked all that way without passing a single clock.

Jesus College: nothing. St Clements church: nothing. Round Church: nothing (although very pretty under a witch's hat of snow). Sidney Sainsbury's: nothing. Nothing along Petty Cury, or even in the grand Arcade. (By the by, where's our red lion? I thought it was coming back – and perhaps it could dangle a clock from its paw.) I know that we have our marvellous and magnificent new chronophage but it's not always on my route and – I'll confess this to you, but don't tell anyone else – I can't actually tell the time from it. The same problem applies to the various sundials dotted around the colleges; I can only assume that they were some early form of graffiti daubed by tourists who visited in the summer and didn't realise that you wouldn't be able to use them to tell the time from September to May. Or perhaps, in the days before anyone needed to set the DVD player or catch a train to London, "November-ish" was as accurate as your time-keeping needed to be.

My reason for going to Johnny Lou-Lou (it's catching) was to buy a mop. And on my way home, I made an interesting discovery: if you carry a mop, people smile at you. I don't know whether it works for all cleaning implements, and it's probably not worth buying one specially. I took care to avoid revolving doors: I had a friend in the City who got his long gentleman's umbrella caught in one, and carried it round for the rest of the day with a right-angle bend in it. Now that did make people smile.

Water, water everywhere

29 March 2010

I'm a sucker for questionnaires and quizzes – can't resist. Promise to match me with my ideal life partner in six questions and I'm hooked. So when I spotted an online test called "How hard is your water?", there I was, popping in my postcode and sharing my intimate clothes-, dish- and hair-washing habits. And it turns out that Cambridge has the Vinnie Jones, nay, the Ray Winstone of water – the hardest in the country. Not for us the delicate velvetiness of Scottish Highlands water, filtered lovingly through mossy banks and stag wee. No, here in East Anglia our water wears knuckle-dusters and laughs raucously if you threaten it with an ASBO (anti-social bathing order).

In practical terms, this means that our washing machines and dishwashers are about 85% limescale. You know that odd chap in the ads who leers at the housewife and then shows her a shiny element? Well, he'd have his work cut out in Cambridge. He'd need more than a piffling little tablet to chip off the towering stalactites of calcium carbonate clinging to our domestic appliances.

Hard water is resistant to soap (rather like teenage boys), so no matter how generous you are with the soap and shampoo, you'll never get a really good lather going here in Cambridge. Bubble bath will make a valiant attempt but die trying, so you won't be able to participate in your own "Carry On"-style lark, with the wife hiding her lover beneath the bubbles when her hubby comes home early for his tea.

Apparently hard water tastes funny – but as I've drunk Cam water for most of my life, I think everyone else's tastes funny. Perhaps I've got limescaled taste-buds. I certainly can't tell the difference when people rave about the varying tastes of bottled waters – I'm just a tap-water girl. That said, I do enjoy the vocabulary that has evolved around bottled water. In Portugal, you ask for water "com gaz" (with gas) or "sem gaz" (without gas), which seems to me to be admirably honest, especially given the effect that carbonated drinks have on my digestion. But here in England we're more coy about it: water can be fizzy or sparkling or lightly carbonated or even (heaven help me – what was I doing in this pretentious place?) joyously effervescent. So perhaps what our local water needs is simple rebranding: it's not hard water, it's strong water – and a lovely Cambridge blue to boot.

Teenagers on tour

9 May 2011

I'm not terribly maternal – never have been. My grandmother used to tell everyone the grisly tale of how I steadily and neatly disembowelled every doll she ever gave me, and one friend still threatens her children with me as a babysitter if they don't behave. And when babies are passed around at family gatherings, you can hear the collective intake of breath when the little mite reaches Auntie Sue – will she drop it or bite it?

It was therefore with mixed feelings – mainly panic and despair – that I greeted the coincidental news from three friends that they were coming to visit Cambridge with their teenage children. In the same week, but thankfully not on the same day. It was a bit like conducting an unreliable sociological experiment, only with less writing and more J20 (which apparently is the beverage du jour of the texting classes). On reflection, I suspect that these nice middle-class parents were hoping that exposure to Cambridge's beauties would encourage their galumphing offspring to work hard at school in order to bag themselves a place here to read whatever those same parents can afford in 2015 (probably a three-week course in intensive vocational call-centre management). Sadly, I fear the plan may have misfired.

It turns out – news to me, but probably not to you – that the average fourteen-year old boy is not blown away by the magnificence of the fan vaulted ceiling in King's chapel (although they perk up at the hefty death toll racked up during its creation). And thirteen year-old girls are similarly not thrilled by the thought of studying in the same city as Sylvia Plath and Shirley Williams – "Who? Is she that loud Welsh singer?". I had slightly more success with other famous graduates – Ali G and Lily Cole seemed to hit the mark.

To a teenager they were horrified at the thought of staying in rooms without en suite facilities (I thought it best not to mention the midwinter cross-quad dash in some colleges), and baffled at the concept of living in one building and going to lectures in another. "Why? And if you can't bring your car up here, how do you get there?" Indeed, transport seemed to be of particular concern to the people carrier generation: the question they all asked was "How long does it take to get to London from here?" Not nearly long enough, as far as I am concerned.

Welcoming Wills and Kate

6 June 2011

Something old, something new… On my wedding day, my old item was my mother's ring, while on Kate Middleton's, she was given Cambridge. I'm not particularly worried – it's not as though she can sidle into a pawn shop with it to tide her over until her next payment from the Privy Purse – but I was amused by the reactions.

Apparently some local people were delighted at the re-creation of the title of Duke of Cambridge because "it puts Cambridge on the map" – suggesting that if we didn't have William, no-one would have heard of our little backwater, nor our world-leading research, hospitals (human and animal), university and, oh, eighty-eight Nobel Prizes. I suppose it might be a handy differentiating shorthand for American tourists, a good number of whom seem to think that Oxbridge is a real place – we're the city belonging to the Duke formerly known as Prince.

So now that we have put each other on the map, we can start thinking about how best to develop this special (dare we suggest essential?) relationship with "our" Royals. They already have a punt named after them, and indeed the privilege of being able to jump to the front of the quayside queue on a busy summer Sunday is not to be sniffed at.

Keeping to the river theme, perhaps we could persuade William and Kate to adopt a pair of the mallards on Jesus Green, to be rechristened the Duck and Duckess of Cambridge. And we could rename the Blue Crew for the Boat Race – perhaps Kate's Eight? – and William could pull a few strings to dig us a shortcut ditch through Duke's Meadows.

The nobility are different to you and me – not least in their peculiar logic that makes the Duke of Devonshire live at Chatsworth while the Duke of Norfolk calls Arundel Castle home. One outcome of this geographical mismanagement is that there are several Duke of Cambridge pubs in London, but none in Cambridge – although we can offer a Fort St George, a Zebra and a Flying Pig, despite our woeful lack of fortifications, African quadrupeds and airborne porkers. So what we really need is a newly named pub, with a helipad in the garden and a suitable brew on tap. A pint of Middleton Mild, your Royal Highness?

A moving story

26 September 2011

The house next door to us is up for sale at the moment. This doesn't happen very often in our street: there are fewer than forty houses to begin with, and the whole street seems to exist in a parallel time-frame not unlike that country club in the movie "Cocoon" (albeit with less golf and a considerably colder swimming pool). We ourselves moved in in 1992 "for a couple of years", and many residents claim a similar spooky inability to leave. So having one of "our" houses on the market really is something of a novelty.

Of course we all dashed – either physically or virtually – to the estate agency to find out the price and to peer at the photos. Strangely for a terraced street, each house is slightly different – and not just internally. A couple have basements, some have converted attics, and one even has a Lilliputian front garden. Purely for sociological research purposes, you understand, it is fascinating to see how each house has developed over the years – for instance, from plain wooden floors to lino, then rugs and shag pile and finally back to plain wood again. So the publication of colour photos is an opportunity not to be missed, and for days now neighbours have greeted each other with "Have you seen what they've done with their boiler cupboard?" and "I like their bathroom fittings".

But the real fun has been The Viewings. To set the scene: our street is in the middle of Cambridge, and the house for sale has four bedrooms. In veterinary terms, this translates to hen's teeth. And not just ordinary hen's teeth, but ones with inlaid diamond chips in the style beloved of New York rappers. The interest has been fevered. Potential buyers have been arriving at fifteen minute intervals, and being right next door – and a nosy moo to boot – I have been in prime position to overhear their pre- and post-viewing comments.

As I stood in my lounge doing the ironing (glamorous to the end), a couple waiting outside my window decided "The neighbours are probably OK – they've got geraniums in their window box.". Heavens – they mean us! I wonder whether criminal profilers are aware of the window box test. As I glowed gently from this approval, the next visitors stood in the same place and boomed "The whole street's a bit poky – I bet everyone can hear what you're saying." Quite.

Fresher pressure

17 October 2011

You know those nature programmes on the telly, the ones where you see a newborn foal or baby giraffe struggling to its feet and taking a few uncertain steps on its nobbly, wobbly legs, its mother watching proudly? Well, it's like that on endless loop in Cambridge city centre at this time of year. The place is full of freshly-scrubbed, wide-eyed first year students, clutching tightly to the new friends they will spend all of next term trying to ditch. Told at interview that it is a legal requirement to ride a bike in Cambridge, they turn up with either (a) a rusting heap that they haven't ridden since they were eight, or (b) a gleaming speed machine that will be stolen within seconds. Regardless of the conveyance, the cycling style will be the same: erratic to the point of danger. Cycling while texting is a new variant not on offer in my day – the closest I got was trying to unwrap and eat a Curly-Wurly while on the wheel.

The second-years meanwhile, released from the stigma of being the new kids, are lolling about, leaning against walls in a louche manner, because it's all just sooooo familiar, and what do you mean you can't find the Sidgwick? They catch sight of friends after four months apart, and indulge in barbed competition about how they spent the summer: "I went kayaking to the source of the Orinoco, then had a month on the beach in Goa." "Oh, did you? I was going to do that, but then I got a summer placement as Nelson Mandela's secretary and couldn't make it – Nelson has *amazing* energy for an old guy."

Considering that we are reputed to attract the cream of Britain's youth to our town, it is surprising how ill-equipped some of them are for life away from mum. I once overheard a lad in Sainsbury's phoning home to ask what ingredients went into beans on toast. On the toast theme, a friend reports that she knew some physics students who blew up their toaster because they buttered the bread before toasting it – otherwise how does the butter melt? And a neighbour says that last week she passed two young bucks standing outside M&S looking in bemusement at people coming out with loaded carrier bags. One turned to the other and said, "You know, I don't think I shall cook at all. I shall just eat out."

Looking for a place

2 May 2016

About this time of year we start getting calls from friends who are coming to Cambridge "for the day". At first we were flattered that so many people wanted to come and see us, but we're wise to it now: it's the season for university visits, and they want somewhere to come for tea and a debrief after the draining round of tours and interviews. Not having children ourselves we're a bit out of the loop on how it all works these days – I just sent in application forms to the places with the nicest-looking brochures and the biggest libraries – but I understand that it is usual for sixth-formers and their parents to attend all sorts of open days at various establishments to find out what is on offer.

You can spot them straight away in town: dad looks both hassled after going round the ring road eight times in search of a car-park and shell-shocked at the price of it when he found it; mum is fidgety in her best non-wedding outfit but trying to look like it's what she wears every day; and their child is trying to keep at least six feet from both of them, while expecting regular injections of food and cash. I remember watching a telly comedy-drama starring Maureen Lipman as just such a mum, set in Cambridge, and it was touching and toe-curling in turns – and made me glad that I came to England alone for university interviews, having informed my parents that NO-ONE's family went with them.

SUSAN IN THE CITY

When I see these little groups bustling around town – consulting a map and wondering in hissed tones whether Trinity and Trinity Hall are the same, and just how you pronounce Caius – I want to go up to them and tell them to do all they can to bag the Cambridge experience. It's an incredibly beautiful and inspiring place to spend three years and – from a parental point of view – the collegiate system and the physically enclosed nature of the town must make this one of the safest places in the world in which to launch that fledgling. I also want to tell them that Cambridge will be colder than you can possibly imagine, that everyone spends the first term expecting to be found out and thrown out, and that the best things you can give your undergraduate child are a Sainsbury's gift card and a sturdy bike lock.

This was the very last column published under the "Susan in the City" byline, on 9 January 2017 – after ten and a half years and 510 columns.

Sexit

9 January 2017

What do these four things have in common: local libraries, fire brigades, the Rio Paralympic Games and me? The answer is that we have all fallen victim to budget cuts, and so this, my 510th weekly column for you, will be my last. Over the years I have had some lovely letters and emails from readers, including one explaining that although she uses old copies of the *Cambridge News* to line her rabbits' cage, she makes sure that my page is never face-up to a leporine bottom. Several people have sent me little presents in response to comments I have made, from article clippings to entire books, and all of these I treasure.

Looking back at the original email discussion I had with then-editor Murray Morse in 2001, I see that he wanted "a female columnist who can write bright, witty, fun, entertaining, off-the-wall, zany, 'I've done that', 'I've thought that', 'that's happened to me', ludicrous, pithy, Bridget Jones' Diary-style, thought-provoking and occasionally controversial stuff" – I hope he would be pleased with how it all turned out (Jaffa Cakes eaten – 3 gazillion).

SUSAN IN THE CITY

In idle moments, I sometimes wondered what might happen if – as Evelyn Waugh imagined in "Scoop" – I were confused with a proper journalist, perhaps a war correspondent, and parcelled off to file my copy from altogether more sinister city locations, perhaps downtown Fallujah or the world's murder capital, Caracas. As Henry Boot did in his column "Lush Places", I could have provided meticulous descriptions of local sights while ignoring the political and military realities of life around me.

So where now for Susan in the City? I will still be she in that I am not leaving Cambridge, but I will no longer be telling you about it every Monday. Instead, as all other candidates fall to the wayside one by one, I hold myself in readiness to be sent to Brussels to lead the Brexit negotiations. Given that no-one admits to having a plan, they could do worse than choose someone who has an organised mind and the ability to meet a deadline, keep to a word count and write clear English. Mind you, I was born in Brussels and so can find my way around, I speak passable French and laughable Flemish, and I'm mad about those spicy speculoo biscuits, so let's face it: I'm vastly over-qualified.

Thank you for reading this book. If you liked what you read, please would you leave a short review on the site where you purchased it, or recommend it to others? Reviews and recommendations are not only the highest compliment you can pay to an author; they also help other readers to make more informed choices about purchasing books.

ABOUT THE AUTHOR

Susan Grossey graduated from Cambridge University in 1987 and since then has made her living from crime. She advises financial institutions and others on money laundering – how to spot criminal money, and what to do about it. She has written many non-fiction books on the subject of money laundering, as well as contributing monthly articles to the leading trade magazine and maintaining a popular anti-money laundering blog.

Her first work of fiction was the inaugural book in the Sam Plank series, "Fatal Forgery". "The Man in the Canary Waistcoat" was her second novel, "Worm in the Blossom" her third, and "Portraits of Pretence" her fourth. Three more Sam Plank mysteries are planned, to complete the series of seven.

Printed in Great Britain
by Amazon